Golf Jokes

The Ultimate Collection of Golfing Jokes

By Chester Croker

Jokes for Golfers

These jokes for golfers will make you laugh out loud. This is quite simply the best collection of the very best golfing jokes and puns around.

There are some great one-liner golf jokes, plenty of questions and answers golf gags, many story led jokes which are designed to be easy to remember, with plenty of risqué golf stories too, some golf slang, some wise golf sayings, a chapter on golf parables, only the best funny golf quotes and as a bonus there are some funnies for junior golfers, and even some corny pick-up lines for golfers too.

All in all, there is something for everyone and these funny golfers jokes are designed to be adapted for your own purposes when with fellow golfers. This huge collection of golf jokes is full of memorable jokes to make you laugh out loud, or snigger to yourself. All in all this book is simply guaranteed to have you in stitches.

Published by Glowworm Press
7 Nuffield Way
Abingdon OX14 1RL

DEDICATION

This book is dedicated to James Day, who has one of the funniest golf swings you are ever likely to see.

He is the man who once told me he takes 17 holes to get warmed up.

He is the man who once told me that one good shank deserves another.

He is the man who once told me he took up golf so he could be useless on weekends too.

He is the man that taught me that no matter how badly you are playing, it is always possible to play worse.

He is the man who, after he missed a short putt, told me it was because his ball was scared of the dark.

For Jim, one birdie is a hot streak.

Jim, you are the inspiration behind this book, and all your golfing buddies salute you.

FOREWORD

When I was approached to write a foreword to this book I was very flattered.

That is until I was told that I was the last resort by the author, Chester Croker, and that everyone else he had asked had said they couldn't do it!

I have known Chester for a number of years and his ability to create funny jokes is absolutely incredible.

He is quick witted and an expert at crafting clever puns and amusing gags and I feel he is the ideal man to put together a golfing joke book. I do remember him once telling me that to see something really funny, I should just watch his short game.

He will be glad you have bought this book, as he has an expensive lifestyle to maintain.

Enjoy!

Major Mulligan

Table of Contents

Chapter 1: Golfing One-Liners

Definition of the game of golf: A five-mile walk punctuated with disappointments.

The game of golf is 90 percent mental and 10 percent mental.

If you think it's hard to meet new people, just pick up the wrong ball on a golf course.

Golf was once a rich man's sport, but now it has millions of poor players.

Golf is an easy game that is just hard to play.

Golf is a game invented by God to punish guys who retire early.

You know you're a hacker when your divot goes further than your ball.

A wife walked into the bedroom and found her husband in bed with his golf clubs. Seeing the astonished look on her face, he calmly said, "Well, you said I had to choose."

He was teed off with his bad shot, driving the ball beyond the green, but he was able to putt it behind him.

Golf is a game in which the slowest people in the world are those in front of you, and the fastest are those behind.

Overheard on the course:-

"It takes a lot of balls to play golf like I do."

The man who takes up golf to get his mind off his work soon takes up work again to get his mind off golf.

I really like the 19th hole. It's the only place I can drink after I drive.

Did you hear about the cross eyed assistant pro who got sacked because he couldn't see eye to eye with his customers.

There are three ways to lower your golf score: take lessons, practise constantly or start cheating.

In primitive society, when people beat the ground with clubs and yelled, it was called witchcraft. Today, in civilized society, it is called golf.

My game is so bad I had to have my ball retriever re-gripped.

Golf is like life - you go for the green, but end up in a hole.

Fairway: [faer-wai]: A tract of closely mown grass running directly from tee to the green. Your ball can usually be found to the left or right of it.

My buddy's golf is improving. He's missing the ball much closer than he used to.

I love playing golf, but when I'm putting I can never catch a break.

I golf in the low 80s.

If it's hotter than that, I won't play.

It's easy to tell a dedicated doctor. He can never understand how a hooker can be happy.

My buddy claims it's no sin to play golf on Sunday. But the way he plays, it is a crime.

Brand new golf balls are attracted to water; and the power of attraction is in direct proportion to how much the balls cost.

Real golfers don't cry when they line up their fourth putt.

My doctor told me to play 18 holes a day, so I went out and bought a harmonica.

The other day I was playing golf and I hit two of my best balls.

I stepped on a rake.

I don't want to excuse him of cheating, but once he had a hole-in-one and scored it as a zero.

I enjoy shooting in the 100's. I figure I'm getting more for my money.

Golf is a game of math and the formula $D=nxP2$ illustrates that the odds of hitting a duffed shot increase by the square of the number of people watching.

I had to change my golfing partner. My last partner would make lots of promises about tee times, but he didn't know how to follow through.

My wife complained about my obsession with golf. I asked her if it was driving a wedge between us.

People who say a shank is close to a perfect shot have never had two in a row.

Good golf etiquette: Always concede the fourth putt.

The 18 handicapper guessed that his ball landed 20 yards off the fairway. Of course, that was just a rough estimate.

If the point of golf is to hit the ball less, then do I win if I don't play at all?

An easy going golfer told his buddy, "I just got a new set of golf clubs for my wife."
His friend replied, "Great trade."

Two fur traders took a golfing trip together. They played a skins match.

Definition of an oxymoron: An easy par three.

Did you hear about the Scotsman who gave up golf after playing for 20 years? He lost his ball.

A golfer with a serious iron deficiency went to the doctor for a check-up and he was told that he was still not out of the woods.

A man who plays golf to forget about work will soon go to work to forget about golf.

Forget about all those "How to play golf better" books, videos and websites. The only sure way to save strokes is with an eraser.

Golf is a game where you yell fore, you get six, and you write five.

Mulligans are the reason golf balls come three to a sleeve.

What are the 3 rules of golf? If the ball goes right it's a slice, if the ball goes left it's a hook, and if the ball goes straight it's a miracle.

Two methods of determining the quality of a golfer's shot can be made by watching acceleration and deceleration - as the club goes back into the bag.

Real golfers don't miss putts, they get robbed.

I am going to divorce my wife because she doesn't understand golf at all. She even thinks Tiger Woods is a forest in India.

Overheard on the course:-

"I didn't miss the putt; the ball missed the hole."

Golf is a game where a ball lies poorly and a golfer lies well.

No, I did not lose my ball. I know where it is. It is in the middle of the lake.

If your opponent has trouble remembering whether he shot a seven or an eight, it means he probably shot a nine.

When it comes to putters, try before you buy. Never buy a putter until you've had a chance to throw it.

At a fancy dress party I bumped into a guy dressed as Luke Skywalker who told me, "Have a good round - may the fours be with you."

There is no shot in golf that is so simple that it can't be messed up.

A hole in one, scored by accident, can keep a complete duffer playing golf for the rest of his life.

A golf widow's lament: - "When I die, I would like to be buried on the golf course so I know that my husband will visit me."

Here's a subtle gag:- "I cannot tell a lie. I always use a caddie."

The reason the pro tells you to keep your head down is so you can't see him laughing.

I played a round of golf today and had two really good drives. To and from the club in my new car.

Our minister is a very good golfer.

Mind you, he's had lots of practise in keeping his head down.

I'm not over the hill. I'm on the back nine.

If nobody knows the trouble you're in, it's probably because they're in the rough on the other side of the hole.

Why is it that the same golfer can't add when it comes to the family budget at home turns into a mathematician on the golf course?

I seldom make the same mistake twice in golf. But then again, I seldom do anything twice in golf.

Yip behind every nervous putter there's a shoulder to cry on.

Golf is so frustrating.

Yesterday, I was just two strokes away from a hole in one.

Chapter 2: Question and Answer Golfer Jokes

Q: Why is the game called "golf"?

A: *Because all the other four letter words were already taken.*

Q: What's the easiest shot in golf?

A: *Your fourth putt.*

Q: What do golf and sex have in common?

A: *They're two things you can enjoy even if you're not very good at either of them.*

Q: How do you find the worst golfer on a golf course?

A: *You just follow the wounded.*

Q: What do most golfers have to shoot to win a tournament?

A: *The rest of the field.*

Q: Are you a scratch golfer?

A: *Yes I am - every time I hit the ball, I scratch my head and wonder where it went.*

Q: What is the difference between driving a car and driving in golf?

A: *When you drive a car you don't want to hit anything.*

Q: What is the difference between a golfer and a fisherman?

A: *When a golfer lies, he doesn't have to bring anything home to prove it.*

Q: What do you call 100 golfers on a stone beach holding hands?

A: *Pebble Beach Golf Links.*

Q: What do you call the perfect golf shot?

A: *A fluke.*

Q: How are golf balls like eggs?

A: *They are white, they are sold by the dozen and a month later you have to buy more.*

Q: Why do golfers put minus signs in front of their scores?

A: *Because subtraction speaks louder than words.*

Q: What's the difference between golfers and the general population?

A: *Fewer people have reached 100.*

Q: What is a true handicap for a good golfer?

A: *Playing against a lousy boss.*

Q: What are the four worst words you could hear during a game of golf?

A: *It's still your turn.*

Q: Where can you find ten doctors all at the same place on any given day?

A: *On the golf course.*

Q: What's the difference between a golf ball and directions?

A: *A man will ask for help looking for a golf ball.*

Q: What should you do if your round of golf is interrupted by a lightning storm?

A: *Walk around holding your 2 iron above your head, because even God can't hit a 2 iron.*

Q: What's the difference between a bad golfer and a bad skydiver?

A: *A bad golfer goes "Whack" then "Damn" whereas a bad skydiver goes "Damn" then "Whack."*

Q: What does a golfer think walking down the middle of the fairway is?

A: *A romantic walk.*

Q: When is the course too wet to play golf?

A: *When your golf cart capsizes.*

Q: What do cricket and golf have in common?

A: *A century is a pretty good score for a bad player in either sport.*

Q: What do bad drivers and bad golfers have in common?

A: *They should both wear a sign that says 'How's My Driving? Call this number.'*

Q: How does a woman prevent her husband from leaving the house?

A: *She hides his golf clubs.*

Q: How is golf like fishing?

A: *Both encourage exaggeration.*

Q: What type of golf game did the fur traders play in the old days?

A: *A skins match.*

Chapter 3: Caddie Jokes

A caddie needs the eyes of a big-game hunter, the strength of a bodybuilder and the patience of a diplomat. If you ever play a top course, especially in the UK, it is recommended that you hire a knowledgeable local caddie to further your enjoyment of the round. Part of the appeal of a caddie is their ability to put anybody in their place with their witty put-downs. Here are without doubt the best caddie gags you will find anywhere.

Golfer: "Golf is a funny game."

Caddie: "It is with you."

Golfer: "I've never played this badly before."

Caddie: "I didn't realize you had played before."

Golfer: "You've got to be the worst caddie in the world."

Caddie: "I doubt it. That would be too much of a coincidence."

Golfer: "How do you like my game?"

Caddie: "It's very good, but personally I prefer golf."

Golfer: "Do you think I can get there with a 6 iron?"

Caddie: "Eventually."

Golfer: "Can you stop looking at your yardage chart – I find it very distracting."

Caddie: "This isn't a yardage chart – it's a map. We're lost."

Golfer: "Would you wade into that stream and see if you can find my ball?"

Caddie: "Why?"

Golfer: "It's my lucky ball."

Golfer: "Just what is the problem with my game?"

Caddie: "You're standing too close to the ball. After you have hit it."

Golfer: "I don't usually play this way."

Caddie: "I should hope not. But tell me, what game do you usually play?"

Golfer: "This can't be my ball. It's too old."

Caddie: "We teed off a long time ago."

Golfer: "Can I drive through those sand traps?"

Caddie: "Only if you were in a tractor."

Golfer: "Can I get home from here?"

Caddie: "Where do you live?"

Golfer: "I'd move heaven and earth to break 100 on this course."

Caddie: "Try heaven. You've already moved most of the earth."

Golfer: "Do you think my game is improving?"

Caddie: "Yes. You miss the ball much closer than you used to."

Golfer: "Do you think it's a sin to play on Sunday?"

Caddie: "The way you play, it's a sin on any day."

Golfer: "This is the worst golf course I've ever played on."

Caddie: "This isn't the golf course. We left that half an hour ago."

Golfer: "I've played so badly all day, I think I'm going to drown myself in that lake."

Caddie: "I'm not sure you could keep your head down that long."

Golfer: "The doctor says I can't play golf."

Caddie: "So he has must have played with you then."

Golfer: "Do you think I can carry that bunker?"

Caddie: "I doubt it. It's got three tons of sand in it."

Golfer: "That's a bad slice."

Caddie: "That's not a slice. That's half the cake."

Golfer: "Tell me something good about my game."

Caddie: "You have a very good short game. Off the tee."

Golfer: "I started so well, but my last few holes have been really bad."

Caddie: "Should I call 911? It looks like you're choking."

Golfer: "That was a really bad putt."

Caddie: "Yes. But at least you had the right club."

Golfer: "Have you noticed any improvement today?"

Caddie: "Yes. You've had your hair cut since I last caddied for you."

Golfer: "I am playing really badly. What do you think I should do?"

Caddie: "Give it up for two weeks."

Golfer: "Then what should I do?"

Caddie: "Give it up for good."

Golfer: "Please stop checking your watch – it's very distracting."

Caddie: "This isn't a watch – it's a compass."

Golfer: "What am I doing wrong?"

Caddie: "Too much loft."

Golfer: "Too much loft?"

Caddie: "Yes, LOFT – Lack Of Flipping Talent."

Caddie: "That's really wild where you have hit your ball – it's what we call 'Lion country'."

Golfer: "What do you mean 'Lion country'?"

Caddie: "If you find it, you're lion!"

Golfer: "I'm ready to go for this green, but there's still a group on the green. What should I do?"

Caddie: "Well, you have two options - you can either go ahead and shank it right now, or wait for the green to clear and then top the ball half way there."

Golfer: "Do you think we'll be able to find my ball?"

Caddie: "You have that hit that ball so far off line, we could wrap that ball in bacon and Lassie still wouldn't be able to find it."

Golfer: "Caddiemaster, that boy isn't even eight years old."

Caddiemaster: "It's better that way, sir. He probably can't count past ten."

Scottish Golfer: "Hey boy, are you any good at finding golf balls?"

Young Caddie: "Yes. I find every lost ball."

Scottish Golfer: "OK. Run and find one, then we can start the round."

Golfer: "I keep striking behind the ball."

Caddie: "Yes, you're striking the course well today."

Golfer: "I want a caddie who can count and keep the score. What's 3 and 4 and 5 add up to?"

Caddie: "Eleven."

Golfer: "Good, you'll do perfectly."

Two caddies are talking to one another while looking for a player's lost ball.

One caddie says to the other, "What sort of a ball was it?"

The other caddie replies, "A brand new one – it's not been hit properly yet."

One caddie says to another, "What's a perk of being a caddie?"

The other caddie replies, "If I have a heart attack on the course, there's always going to be a doctor nearby."

On the third green a meticulous player was studying the green. He got down on his hands and knees to check out the turf between his ball and the hole. He flicked several pieces of grass out of the way and after standing up, he held up a wet finger to establish the direction and strength of the wind. Turning to his caddie he asked, "Was the green mowed this morning?"

The caddie replied, "Yes, sir."

The golfer asked, "Right to left or left to right?"

The caddie replied, "Right to left, sir."

The golfer putted; and missed the hole completely. He whirled on the caddie and yelled, "What TIME was it cut?"

A golfer and his caddie walk up to a long par 3.

The cocky golfer says, "Looks like a 3 iron and a putter."

The caddie hands him the 3 iron and the golfer tops his ball about fifty yards in front of him.

The caddie immediately hands him his putter and says, "Good luck with that putt."

In court, a judge asked a man in the witness box, "Do you truly understand the seriousness of things when you swear and state an oath?"

The man replied, "Do I ever, your honor - I once caddied for you!"

Caddying for the elderly golfer had required great patience. The mature golfer had sworn to break 100 before the summer was out. In fact there was a bottle of malt whisky riding on it which his caddie would receive when the century had been broken.

A day arrived when his dogged persistence seemed about to pay off.

They were on the green at the eighteenth and 97 strokes had already been accounted for.

Both the player and caddie were excited and in the grip of such emotion it was small wonder that the player sent his first putt racing ten feet past the hole.

In a flash the caddie dropped the flagstick, picked up the ball and excitedly said, "Well done, sir. You've done it! Anyone would give you that putt."

One day, a Jewish guy went to play a golf course that advertised they could supply caddies of all types and that they could meet special requirements.

When he arrived at the clubhouse he told the Caddie Master that he wanted a caddie that worked in the Jewish style.

This surprised the Caddie Master, who had never heard of that requirement before.

Anyway, he called all his caddies together and asked if anyone could help.

After a long silence, a new caddie sitting in a corner said he could.

On the way to the first tee the new caddie said, "Actually, I do not know how to caddie in the Jewish style, but since I am new I wanted to impress the other caddies. If you teach me how to do it I will only charge half the fee."

The Jewish guy said, "You learn fast."

Many a golfer prefers a golf cart to a caddie because it cannot count, criticize or laugh.

The golfer had a terrible lie in the woods, with his ball deep in thick rough and wedged between two tree roots.

He considered the situation for a minute and then turned to his caddie and said, "You know what shot I'm going to take here?"

"Yes, sir." replied the caddie as he passed him a hip flask of malt whisky.

A caddie was particularly nice to me after I hit my best drive of the day when he said to me, "Och, I don't go that far on holiday."

A young caddie came running into the pro shop saying, "Mrs McDougall has been stung by a bee."

The pro asked where and the caddie replied, "Between the first and second hole."

The pro calmly said, "Tell her that her stance is too wide."

I was playing golf in Africa once, and my caddie had a rifle, which he said he carried in case of wild animals.

On the 3rd hole I was just about to hit a wedge when a leopard leapt out at me. "Bang" the caddie shot it.

On the 7th hole I was lining up a putt when a crocodile made a move for me. "Bang" the caddie shot it.

On the 12th hole I was walking up to the green and I could see a lion. I didn't worry as I figured that the caddie would sort it out.

The lion started getting closer and the caddie still hadn't shot it. The lion got closer and then started running towards me. I shouted to the caddie to shoot it, but he said, "No Sir, you don't get a shot on this hole."

A visiting golfer at St. Andrews was having a miserable round when he hit his fourth shot into the infamous bunker guarding the green on the Road Hole.

"What do I do now?" he asked his caddie.

"Well, sir, The Jigger Inn is just down the road," the caddie said. "I think we should go there, have a wee drink and rethink the whole thing."

Shamus was a reasonable golfer but he had a reputation for being poor with his bunker shots.

One day, he took a caddie who became exasperated at Shamus's shameful efforts during the round.

On the eighteenth hole, Shamus played his ball into a deep fairway bunker and he asked his caddie what club he should use.

His frustrated caddie replied, "Never mind the club. Just take plenty of food and water."

Chapter 4: Shorter Golfer Jokes

You can easily change the names in here to suit your own story telling purposes.

Terry stood over his tee shot for what seemed an eternity; looking up, looking down, measuring the distance, figuring the wind direction and speed.

Finally his exasperated partner says, "What's taking so long?"

Terry answers, "My wife is up there watching me from the clubhouse. I want to make this a perfect shot."

His partner says, "Forget it, man. You don't stand a snowball's chance in hell of hitting her from here!"

Four golfers were introducing themselves to one another on the first tee.

One asked, "How do you feel about a lot of swearing and moaning?"

"It doesn't bother me at all," answered another.

"Good" replied the golfer who had asked the question, "In which case would you like to telephone my wife and tell her where I am."

A hacker hit a dreadful slice off the tee that ricocheted through the trees and onto an adjoining fairway, narrowly missing another golfer.

When he got to his ball, he was greeted by the unintentional target, who angrily told him of the near miss.

"I'm very sorry" the errant golfer said, "I didn't have time to shout fore."

"That's odd" the man replied," you had plenty of time to shout sh*t."

It's a foggy day, and two dim-witted golfers are teeing off on a par 3. They both tee off, and proceed to the green to find their balls.

One ball is about four feet from the cup while the other has found its way into the cup for a hole-in-one. Both were playing the same type of balls and the same number, Titleist 3, but they couldn't determine which ball was which, and who had made the hole in one.

They decided to ask the golf pro to help them out.

After congratulating both golfers on their fine shots, the golf pro asks, "Which one of you used the orange ball?"

Glynn and Liam emerged from the clubhouse to tee off at the first hole.

"Anything the matter, mate?" Liam asked his buddy.

"I really can't stand the new club pro," Glynn replied "he's just been trying to correct my stance."

Liam soothed, "He's only trying to help your game."

Glynn replied, "Yeah, but I was using the urinal at the time."

An American citizen is vacationing on his own in Scotland.

He decides to play a round of golf and is paired with three local gents.

On the first hole he hooks his tee shot out of bounds.

He shakes his head, reaches into his pocket, and re-tees another ball.

He strikes this one down the middle of the fairway.

With a big smile, he says to the others, "In the U.S., we call that a Mulligan; I was wondering what you called it here in Scotland."

One of the locals replies, "Hitting three."

Dan said to Tim, "I discovered something really important about golf today. I discovered that I should study the marker that is posted by the tee box very carefully."

Tim asked, "Does that help you choose the right club to play?"

Dan replied, "No, it helps me play the right hole."

A mixed foursome is on the first tee.

"It's raining a little today," the husband stated. "You and I aren't bothered by a little rain, are we?"

"Why is he telling you not to be bothered by a little rain?" the other woman said to his wife.

"He's not talking to me," the wife replied, "He's talking to his golf bag."

A golf professional was approached by two women in the pro shop.

"Do you wish to learn to play golf, madam?" he asked one of the ladies.

Oh, no," she replied, "it's my friend who's interested in learning. I learned last Wednesday."

A tall highlander walked into the pro shop at Pitlochry Golf Club and stood ramrod straight as he pulled a badly nicked ball from his sporran.

"What can you do with this?" he asked the golf pro.

"Well," said the pro, "we can vulcanise it for twenty pence or re-cover it for fifty."

"I'll let ye know t'morra," said the Highlander.

The next day he was back, holding out the ball, and said to the pro, "The Regiment has voted to vulcanise it."

A hacker called Patrick tells his pals, "I'll always remember the day I beat ninety for the first time. I had a few beers in the clubhouse and was so pleased with myself I chose to skip playing the back nine."

During the weekly childbirth meeting, the room was full of pregnant women and their partners.

The breathing and relaxation techniques class was in full swing, when the instructor announced, "Ladies, exercise is good for you. Walking is especially beneficial. And, gentlemen, it wouldn't hurt you to take the time to go walking with your partner."

From the back of the room one expectant father inquired, "Would it be okay if she carries a bag of golf clubs while she walks?"

A murder has been committed and the police had been called to an apartment where they found a man holding a 9 iron in his hand, looking at the lifeless body of a woman on the floor.

The detective asks, "Sir, is that your wife?"

The guy replies, "Yes."

The detective asks, "Did you hit her with that golf club?"

The guy replies, "Yes, yes I did."

The man than stifles a sob, drops the club and puts his hands on his head.

The detective asks, "How many times did you hit her?"

The guy replies, "I'm not sure. Five, six, seven? Put me down for a five."

Colin tells his buddy off saying, "You're late on the tee, Gary."

Gary replied, "Yes, as it's a Sunday, I had to toss a coin to see if I should go to church or go and play golf."

Colin says, "Okay, but why are you so late?"

Gary replied, "I had to toss the coin five times."

"Sometimes my husband fades the ball, sometimes he draws it," one wife said to another as they waited to tee off.

"How does he decide which shot to play?" said the other wife.

"It depends," his wife replied as her husband hit the ball into the rough on the left of the hole.

"That was a draw," she told her friend.

She continued, "If he wanted to be in the rough on the right side of the hole, then he would have faded it."

When a woman wears a leather dress, a man's heart beats quicker, his throat gets dry, he goes weak at the knees, and he begins to think irrationally.

Ever wonder why?

It's probably because she smells like a new golf glove.

I was asked, "Has your swing changed much over the years?"

I replied, "It hasn't changed much, but it sure has changed often."

Dave is at the altar on his wedding day. By his side are his golf bag and clubs.

His bride whispers, "What are your golf clubs doing here?"

Dave replies, "Well this isn't going to take all day, is it?"

Two golfers are in the bar after a round of golf.

Will asks his buddy, "You made a 9 on a par 3? How did you manage that?"

Jim replies, "I chipped in from the fringe."

As a couple approaches the altar, the groom tells his wife-to-be, "Honey, I've got something to confess. I am a golf nut, and every chance I get, I'll be playing golf."

"Since we're being honest," replies the bride, "I have to tell you that I'm a hooker."

The groom replies, "That's okay, honey. You just need to learn to keep your head down and your left arm straight."

A golfer sliced a ball into a field of chickens, striking one of the hens and killing it instantly. He was understandably upset, and sought out the farmer.

"I'm sorry," he said, "my terrible tee-shot hit one of your hens and killed it. Can I replace the hen?"

"I doubt it," replied the farmer, mulling it over. "How many eggs a day do you lay?"

A wife complains to her husband, "You spend so much time thinking about golf. Do you even remember our last wedding anniversary?"

The husband replies, "Of course, I do darling. It was the same day I sank that 60 foot putt."

At a petrol station in rural Ireland, a Rolls Royce pulled up, driven by a well-dressed man in his golf attire. As he went to pay for his fuel, a couple of tees fell out of his pocket.

When the attendant asked what they were for, the golfer said, "They are for resting my balls on when I am driving."

The attendant sighed and said, "Rolls Royce really do think of everything."

Two golfers are in the bar after a round of golf.

Derek asks, "How bad do you want to be a good golfer?"

Bryan replies, "I have a driving ambition."

A fourball were putting on the fifth green, as a single player played up short of the green.

As they teed off on the next hole, they noticed him quickly chip on and putt out, before running up to their tee.

Sensing their bewilderment, he said, "Sorry, do you mind if I play through - I've just heard that my wife has had a terrible accident and I need to get home urgently."

A guy is on the first tee - a long par 3 over water and the pro advises him to hit a brand new Titleist Pro V1.

The guy tees up the Titleist and takes a couple of practice swings.

The pro says to him, "On second thoughts, hit a range ball."

A bad tempered golfer was nicknamed Tomahawk after he had earnt a reputation for throwing golf clubs around after playing bad shots.

He decided it was time to upgrade his clubs and so he bought a new set of Taylor Made R19 irons.

After playing with them for a couple of rounds he told his buddies, "These are the best clubs I have ever had. In fact, I can throw these clubs twenty yards further than my old ones."

An Irish guy is on vacation and after his round goes into the clubhouse.

The head pro says, "Did you have a good time out there?"

The Irishman replied, "Fabulous, thank you."

The pro said, "How did you find the greens?"

The Irish guy replied, "Easy. I just walked to the end of the fairways and there they were."

A wife complains to her husband, "I'm sick and tired of your obsession with golf."

The husband replies, "Why? Is it driving a wedge between us?"

A husband and wife go to a marriage counselor as their marriage is having major difficulties.

The counselor asks them what the problem is and the wife goes into a rage, listing every problem they have had in the twenty years they've been married, and she goes on and on and on.

The counselor stands up, walks around the desk and embraces the woman, kissing her passionately.

The woman shuts up and sits down quietly in a daze.

The counselor turns to the husband and says, "That is what your wife needs at least three times a week, can you do that?"

The husband says, "No I can't. I play golf on Mondays and Fridays, but I can bring her in for you on Wednesdays."

Two golfers are in the bar after a round of golf.

Sean tells Lee, "I was one under today."

Lee says, "What?"

Sean replies, "Yes, I was one under a tree, one under a bush and one under a cart."

Two golfers are in the bar after a round of golf.

Stewart tells his buddy, "I played World War II golf today - out in 39 and home in 45."

Shaun says, "I played Civil War golf today - out in 61 and home in 65."

Doug is struggling with his putting on the first few holes and complains, "I've got a case of the yips. I just can't seem to putt at all. It must be my nerves or maybe it's because I'm getting older."

"Nope," said his golfing buddy Dave, "It's probably because you had a few pints of beer before you went out to play."

My stockbroker is a golf nut.

One day he called me up and said, "Guess what? I just broke 80."

I said, "I know. I'm one of them."

Two golfers are ready to play on the 14th tee as a funeral cortege passes by. Bill doffs his cap, and bows his head as the cortege passes.

"That was a really nice thing to do," his mate Ben says. "It's good to see there is still some respect in the world."

"Well, it's only right," Bill replies. "I was married to her for 20 years."

***

It is pouring with rain and two longtime golf buddies were standing on a tee box overlooking a river, and are getting ready to hit their tee shots.

One of them pointed up the river, turned to the other and said, "Just look at those fools fishing in this rain."

***

"Do you pay a high price to play golf here?" a golfer was asked as he left the club house.

"I will today," the golfer replied. "I didn't tell my wife I was coming here."

Adrian hit his ball into the trees.

His pal heard 'whack, whack, whack' over and over again, until finally he got the ball out.

His pal asked, "How many strokes did it take you to get out of there?"

Adrian replied, "Three."

His pal then said, "I heard seven."

Adrian exclaimed, "Four of them were echoes."

On a visit to the fortune teller a golfer asks, "Are there golf courses in Heaven?"

The fortune teller replies, "I have some good news, and I have some bad news."

The golfer asked, "So what's the good news?"

The fortune teller said, "The good news is that Heaven's golf courses are beautiful beyond anything you could imagine."

The golfer asked, "What's the bad news?"

The fortune teller replied, "You have a tee-time at 8:30a.m next Sunday morning."

A couple of elderly gents were golfing when one said he was going to Dr. Wilson for a new set of dentures in the morning.

His friend remarked that he had gone to the same dentist a few years before.

"Is that so?" the first guy said. "Did he do a good job?"

His friend said, "Well, I was playing the tenth hole yesterday when a fellow on the ninth hole hooked a shot.2

His friend continued, "The ball must have been going 100 mph when it hit me in the groin, and that was the first time in two years my teeth haven't hurt."

Mike and Jimmy are playing a challenging course and as usual Mike is having a tough time off the tee.

On the 6th hole he hits a huge slice.

Mike asks, "Did you see where that drive went? Is it in the deep rough?"

Jimmy says, "Yes."

Mike asks, "How far in?"

Jimmy replies, "I'm not sure, but I hope our cart has 4-wheel drive."

Dan set up his ball on a tough par five, took a mighty swing and hit his drive into a clump of trees.

He found his ball and saw an opening between two trees he thought he could hit through. He took a big swing with his 3-wood and the ball hit a tree, bounced back, hit him on the forehead and killed him instantly.

As he approached the gates of Heaven, St. Peter saw him coming and asked, "Are you a good golfer?"

Dan replied, "I got here in two, didn't I?"

An alien spaceship silently hovered over a golf course and the aliens inside watched a solitary golfer in wonder.

The golfer topped his tee shot, sliced his second into the deep rough, took three shots to get his ball out of the rough back onto the fairway, shanked the next shot into the bushes, and he then took four more shots to get it out on the fairway again.

The golfer then thinned the ball into a bunker. He took several more shots to get out of the bunker and eventually onto the green. He putted several times until he finally got it into the hole.

At this point, one alien said to another, "Wow, now he is in serious trouble."

A woman goes into her local newspaper office to get an obituary for her recently deceased husband published.

The obituary editor informs her that there is a charge of a dollar per word.

She pauses, reflects, and then says, "Well then, let it read 'Steve Daniels died.'"

The editor tells her that there is a seven word minimum for all obituaries.

She thinks it over and then says, "In that case, let it read, 'Steve Daniels died: golf clubs for sale.'"

Joe and his priest are playing a match.

Joe's game is faultless, and he is giving the priest a thorough pasting.

After they have played the final hole, the priest sighs as he fills in the scorecard.

Sensing his pastor's discomfort, Joe says to him, "Cheer up Father - just think, one of these days you will be giving the services at my funeral."

The Priest looked at him and made a poor attempt at a grin while saying, "Yes, that may well be true, but it will still be your hole."

Colin addressed the ball and took a magnificent swing but somehow, something went wrong and a horrible slice resulted.

The ball went onto the adjoining fairway and hit a man on the head who dropped to the ground immediately.

Colin and his partner ran up to the suffering victim who was lying unconscious with the ball between his feet.

Colin exclaimed, "Crikey, what shall I do?"

"Don't move him" said his partner, "if we leave him here he becomes an immovable obstruction and you can either play the ball as it lies or take a two club length penalty drop."

MacDermott and MacDuff were sitting in the clubhouse on a raw, blustery day, thawing their beards in front of the fireplace while freezing rain was beating against the windows.

The pair were silent for a long time over their whiskys.

Finally, MacDermott spoke, "That was quite a round of golf."

MacDuff replied, "Same time next Saturday?"

"Aye," said MacDermott, "weather permitting."

A group of four golfers stood on the tee of the 441 yards par 4 sixteenth hole.

There was a road that ran alongside the hole on the left hand side.

The first golfer teed off and hooked his tee shot into the road where it bounced 150 yards down the road, until it hit the tire of a moving bus and was knocked back onto the golf course stopping just 10 yards short of the green.

As they all stood in amazement, a fellow golfer asked, "How on earth did you do that?"

The response came without hesitation, "You have to know the bus schedule."

James was playing a round of golf with the club pro one day and after a few holes he asked the pro, "What do you think of my game?"

The pro replied, "You should shorten your clubs by two inches."

James asked, "Do you think that would help my game?"

The pro replied, "No, but it will help them fit in the trash can."

Two Mexican detectives were investigating the murder of Juan Gonzalez.

The first detective asked, "How was he killed?"

The second detective replied, "He was shot with a golf gun."

The first detective asked, "A golf gun? What's a golf gun?"

The second detective replied, "I'm not sure, but it made a hole in Juan."

Two women were put together as partners in the club tournament and met on the putting green for the first time.

After introductions, the first golfer asked the other, "What's your handicap?"

"Oh, I'm a scratch golfer," the other replied.

"Really?" exclaimed the first woman, suitably impressed that she was paired up with her.

The other woman replied, "Yes, I write down all my good scores and scratch out the bad ones!"

A hot shot lawyer sent gifts to some of his clients. The gifts were sleeves of golf balls, inscribed with the lawyer's name.

One of the recipients sent an email of thanks to the lawyer saying, "That's the first time I've ever had a lawyer buy the balls."

Two competitive Scots, Jock and Jimmy, come upon a water hole.

Jock tees up and hits it into the middle of the lake.

He reaches into his bag to find that he is out of balls.

He then asks Jimmy for a ball who gives him one of his spare balls out of his bag.

Jock then proceeds to hit that ball into the lake as well.

This goes on twice more and when he asks Jimmy for yet another ball, Jimmy says, "Jock, these balls cost me a pretty penny."

Jock replies, "Och, Jimmy if you cannee afford to play the game, ya should nee be oot here."

Two friends were having a discussion on why they like the game of golf.

"What I like about golf," the first guy said, "is that you get to spend the day outdoors in the sun and fresh air, exercising your body and mind."

His friend said, "I'll tell you why golf is such a great game. Where else can a guy like me get to spend the day with a bunch of hookers and not have his wife kill him."

A male golfer playing in a mixed foursomes alternate shot tournament hit his tee shot to the edge of the green on a short par 3.

His female partner, playing the second shot, managed to chip it over the green into a bunker.

Undaunted, the guy recovers with a fine shot to within three feet of the hole.

The lady golfer nervously putts, and sends the ball one foot past the hole, leaving the guy to sink the return putt.

As they are walking off the green, the guy said, "Do you realize that we took five strokes on an easy par 3?"

His partner replied, "Yes, and don't forget who took three of them."

Father O'Reilly was playing golf with a parishioner.

On the first hole, the priest sliced his ball into the rough. His opponent heard the priest mutter "Hoover" under his breath.

On the second hole, the ball went straight into a water hazard.

He said, "Hoover" again, a little louder this time.

On the third hole, Father O'Reilly's putt edged the hole rather than going in.

"Hoover" he said again.

His opponent couldn't withhold his curiosity any longer, and asked, "Why do you say "Hoover" after a bad shot."

The priest replied, "It's the biggest dam I know."

Dave and Brian were getting ready to tee off on the first hole when Brian noticed that Dave had got a new set of irons.

Brian asked Dave how he liked the clubs and if they've helped his game at all.

Dave replied, "They're great clubs. They've added at least 20 yards to my slices, about 30 yards to my hooks and you would be amazed at the size of my divots now!"

Three men are in a bar, bragging about their families.

The first guy says, "I have four sons. One more and I'll have a basketball team."

The second guy says, "That's nothing. I have ten sons. One more and I'll have a cricket team."

The third guy replies, "You guys haven't found true happiness. I have seventeen wives. One more and I'll have a golf course."

A guy visits his local golf pro for a complete beginners lesson, explaining that he knew nothing whatever of the game.

The pro showed him the stance and swing, and then said, "Just hit the ball towards the flag on the first green."

The novice teed up and struck the ball straight as a dye onto the green, where it stopped a few feet from the hole.

"Now what?" the fellow asked the speechless pro.

After he was able to speak again the pro said, "You're supposed to hit the ball into the cup."

"Oh great. NOW you tell me," said the beginner in a disgusted tone.

Golf tour manager Mikey went with his colleague Bryan to check out a course they had not played before, which came with a reputation for being really hard.

Bryan teed up on the first hole, addressed the ball, took a couple of waggles and took a swing.

He hit a foot behind the ball, made a huge divot and totally missed the ball.

Unphased he stepped back, took a couple of practice swings, addressed his ball, swung, missed everything and took yet another huge divot.

He stepped back from his ball again and said to Mikey, "This is a really tough course!"

A fellow comes home after his regular Saturday golf game and his wife asks him why he doesn't play with Paul Thomas any more.

The husband said, "Would you want to play with a guy who regularly cheats, swears up a storm over everything, lies about his score, and has nothing good to say about anyone else on the course - ever?"

"Of course I wouldn't," replies the wife.

"Well," says the husband, "neither does Paul Thomas."

Two golfers are waiting their turn on the tee when a naked women runs across the course and into the woods.

Two men in white coats and another man carrying two buckets of sand are chasing her, and a little old man is bringing up the rear.

One of the golfers grabs the old man and asks, "What's going on?"

The old guy says, "She's a nymphomaniac from the asylum, she keeps escaping, and we are trying to catch her."

The golfer says, "What about the guy with the buckets of sand?"

The old guy says, "That's his handicap. He caught her last time."

A father told his son, "The time has come for you and I to have a conversation. Soon, you will have new urges and feelings that you have not had before and that will be hard for you to understand. Your heart will pound and your hands will sweat. You'll be pre-occupied and won't be able to think of anything else."

He added, "But don't worry, it's perfectly normal; it's called golf."

"You surely don't want me to hole that?" an irritating 8 handicapper called Clive blustered.

His ball was about a foot from the cup and his opponent answered quietly, "No."

Clive picked up his ball and they both walked onto the next tee.

Clive was about to place his ball onto the tee when he was interrupted by his opponent who said, "I think you will find it is my honor; I won the last hole, as you picked up and didn't putt out."

"But you said you didn't want me to hole out," spluttered Clive.

"That is right. I didn't, and you didn't." said his opponent.

"When can I have another lesson?" a golfer asked his pro - a veteran at 70 years of age.

"Tomorrow morning," came the reply, "but not in the afternoon. That's when I visit my father."

"Goodness me," exclaimed the student in amazement, "how old is he?"

The pro replied, "95."

The student asked, "Is he a good player too?"

The pro replied, "He is ok, bless him, but he'll never make it to the top level."

One sunny afternoon, a single player was added to a couple's golf game.

After a few holes the couple finally asked him why he was playing alone.

He replied that he and his wife played this course every year for 20 years, but this year she died and he wanted to keep the tradition going in her honor.

The emotional couple wondered if there were any friends or family who would have liked to play with him today.

He responded, "I asked myself that same question, but they all preferred to go to the funeral."

A junior golfer was questioning scratch golfer and club legend Lee Black.

The youngster says, "You are a great golfer. You really know your way around the course. What is your secret?"

Lee replied, "It's simple. The holes are numbered."

A young man and a priest are playing together. At a short par 3 the priest asks, "What are you going to use on this hole, my son?"

The young man says, "An eight iron, Father. How about you?"

The priest says, "I'm going to hit a soft seven iron and pray."

The young man hits his eight iron and his ball lands on the green.

It is the priest's turn, but he tops his seven iron and the ball dribbles into the greenside bunker.

The young man says, "I don't know about you, Father, but in my church, when I pray, I keep my head down."

"I heard that you earn more than our Prime Minister," one member told his club pro.

The pro replied, "I'm a better player than he is."

I saw a green keeper on the second hole today slumped over his lawn mower, crying his eyes out.

I asked him if he was OK.

He replied, "I'm just going through a rough patch."

A man and his wife walked into a dentist's office.

The man said to the dentist, "I'm in a hurry. I have two buddies waiting for us to play golf. . I just don't have time to wait for the anesthetic to work. So let's forget about the anesthetic and just pull the tooth and be done with it."

The dentist thought to himself, "My goodness, this is a very brave man, asking me to pull his tooth without using anything to kill the pain."

So the dentist asked him, "Which tooth is it, sir?"

The man turned to his wife and said, "Open your mouth, Honey, and show the dentist which tooth hurts."

A priest was halfway down the first fairway, waiting to hit his second shot, when he heard "Fore!" and a ball slammed into his back.

The golfer who had hit the ball was soon on the scene to offer his apologies.

When the priest assured him that he was all right, the man smiled.

"Thank goodness, Father," he exclaimed. "I've been playing this game for forty years, and I have finally hit my first holy one."

Eddie and Liam meet on the golf course and decide to finish off the round together. Eddie has a little dog with him and on the next green, when Eddie holes out with a 20 foot putt the little dog starts woofing and stands up on its hind legs.

Liam is amazed at this clever trick and says, "That dog is really talented. What does it do if you miss a putt?"

Eddie replies, "Somersaults."

Liam exclaims, "Wow - somersaults! How many does it do?"

Eddie calmly replies, "It depends on how hard I kick it up the ass."

An American and a Scot were talking about playing golf during the various seasons of the year.

"In most parts of the USA we cannot play in the winter time. We have to wait until spring," the American said.

"In Scotland we play in the winter time. Snow and cold are no object to us," said the Scot.

"Well, what do you do; paint your balls black?" asked the American.

"No," said the Scot "we just put on an extra sweater."

Matthew was not having a good day at the golf course. After he missed a twelve inch putt, his partner asked him what the problem was.

"It's the wife," said Matt. "As you know, she's taken up golf, and since she's been playing, she's cut my sex down to once a week."

"Well you should think yourself lucky," said his partner. "She's cut me out altogether."

Every time the man next door headed towards Charlie's house it was to borrow something.

"He won't get away with it this time," muttered Charlie to his wife. "Watch this."

The neighbor said, "I wonder if you'd be using your power-saw this morning."

"I'm very sorry," said Charlie with a smug look, "but the fact of the matter is, I'll be using it all day."

"In that case," said the neighbor, "you won't be using your golf clubs, so do you mind if I borrow them?"

A forty-something single enthusiastic golfer was browsing an online dating site called Singles247.com when he came across an interesting profile from an attractive lady living in the same town as him.

The profile read as follows - Slim, attractive, buxom blonde, 5' 6", successful in business, happy in life, great sense of humor, no children (or desire to have them), enjoys traveling, pampering her man and the finer things in life. Seeks similar qualities in a partner for long term relationship. Golfers need NOT apply.

The husband says to his wife, "My doctor just told me that I should give up golf."

His wife asks, "Why? Did he look at your knees?"

The husband replies, "No, he looked at my scorecard."

Two couples went out golfing together.

The men hit first from the men's tee and walked with the ladies to their tee box.

The first lady took a mighty swing at the ball, missing it completely, while passing some gas rather loudly in the process.

No one commented.

She addressed the ball again but this time she passed just a little gas as she made contact with the ball, topping it and moving it only a short distance.

She said, "I wonder why it didn't go any further?"

One of the men said, "I don't think you gave it enough gas!"

A young golfer was at his first golf lesson when he asked the pro, "Is the word spelled put or putt?"

The pro replied, "P-U-T means to place something where you want it whereas P-U-T-T means a futile attempt to do the same thing."

A newly wed woman said to her husband, "Honey, now that we are married, I would like you to play golf once a week instead of twice."

He said, "You are beginning to sound like my ex-wife.

She said, "I didn't know you were married before."

He said, "I wasn't!"

Ed and Emma met while on a cruise, and they fell head over heels in love with one another.

On the last night of their vacation, the two went to dinner and had a serious talk about their potential future relationship.

"It's only fair to warn you, I'm a total golf nut," Ed said to his new lady friend. "I eat, sleep and breathe golf, so if that's a problem, you'd better say so now."

Emma responded, "If we're being honest with each other, here goes - I'm a hooker."

"I see," Ed replied, and was quiet for a moment.

Ed then said, "You know, it's probably because you're not keeping your wrists straight."

Paddy sliced his tee shot deep into a wooded ravine on the seventh hole.

He took his seven iron and clambered down the embankment in search of his ball.

After many minutes of hacking at the undergrowth, he spotted something glistening in the leaves.

As he got closer, he discovered what he saw was a seven iron in the hands of a skeleton.

Paddy immediately called out to his partner, "Alex, I've got a major problem down here."

"What's the matter?" Alex asked from the edge of the ravine.

Paddy replied, "Bring me my wedge. You can't get out of here with a seven iron."

Shaun is not the brightest individual.

One day he popped into the Pro shop to see if he could get a bargain.

The assistant pro showed him a set of clubs, and said, "These clubs will cut your handicap by 50%."

Shaun replied, "That sounds good. I'll take two sets."

A visitor was trying to book a round of golf and the club secretary was apologetic saying, "I'm sorry, Sir, but we have no tee times available on the course today."

The visitor said, "What if I told you Prince Andrew wanted a game today. Could you find a tee time for him?"

The secretary replied, "Yes, of course I would."

The visitor rejoined, "I happen to know that he's out of the country at the moment, so I'll take his tee time."

A dentist was a very keen golfer and would often take time off work to play a round.

One day, he told his secretary to cancel all his appointments, and to leave the following message on the answer phone:

"Dr. Paine is fully occupied today as he needs to fill 18 cavities. Please ring tomorrow for an appointment. Thank you."

A blonde golfer goes into the pro shop and says, "I want some green golf balls."

The pro looks all over the shop, checks a couple of websites, and finally calls his main supplier and establishes that sure enough, there are no green golf balls.

As the blonde golfer leaves, the pro asks her, "Before you go, could you tell me why you want green golf balls?"

She replies, "Because they would be easier to find in the sand traps."

A young Edinburgh minister was playing in a match at North Berwick.

He had a short putt for the half and not knowing the subtle etiquette of golf, he was walking off as if the putt had been holed.

The adversary demurred to this and the minister proceeded to miss his short putt.

"No gentleman," he remarked, "would have asked me to hole a short putt like that."

"Maybe not," said the adversary calmly, "but in this case we are not gentlemen, we are golfers."

The old Scottish golfer paced up and down outside the emergency room at Roodlands Hospital, near Gullane Golf Links.

Inside, doctors were trying to remove a golf ball accidentally driven down a player's throat.

The sister in charge noticed the elderly golfer, and went to reassure him.

She said, "It's under control. Hopefully it won't be long. Are you a relative?"

The old Scot replied, "No. It's my ball."

Four old friends met on Sunday morning for a round of golf.

One wheezed, "These hills get steeper as the years go by."

The second gasped, "The rough seem to be getting longer."

The third complained, "The greens seem to be getting smaller."

The fourth, the wisest of the group, counselled them saying, "Let's all be thankful we're still on this side of the grass."

Chapter 5: Longer Golfer Jokes

Remember, that the names used in this book are the products of the author's imagination or used in a fictitious manner. Any resemblance to actual persons, living or dead is purely coincidental.

You can easily change any of the names to suit your own story telling purposes.

What's In A Lie

Bob, a 70 year-old, extremely wealthy widower, shows up at the country club with a breathtakingly beautiful and very sexy 25 year-old blonde.

She hangs onto Bob's arm and listens intently to his every word.

His buddies at the club are all aghast.

At the very first chance, they corner him and ask, "Bob, where did you get the trophy girlfriend from?"

Bob replies, "Girlfriend? She's my wife!"

They're amazed, but ask, "So, how did you persuade her to marry you?"

Bob replies, "I lied about my age."

The pals ask, "Did you tell her you were only 50?"

Bob smiles and says, "No, I told her I was 90."

Locker Room Call

Several men are in the locker room of a golf club.

A cell phone on a bench rings and one of the guys responds by activating the speakerphone.

All the others stop to listen.

Man: "Hello."

Woman: "Honey, it's me, are you at the club?"

Man: "Yes."

Woman: "I'm at the mall and I found a very nice leather jacket for only 900 dollars. Do you think I should buy it?"

Man: "Of course you should buy it."

Woman: "I went to the Mercedes showroom and the manager showed me a car that I really like."

Man: "How much?"

Woman: "75,000 dollars."

Man: "OK, that's fine."

Woman: "Fantastic. I will see you later Honey. I love you."

Man: "I love you too."

The man hangs up, smiles, looks around and asks, "Does anyone know who this mobile phone belongs to?"

Sucker

A fellow is getting ready to tee-off on the first hole when a second guy approaches and asks if he can join him.

The first says that he usually plays alone but agrees to let the second guy join him. After the first couple of holes they are even and the second guy says, "We're about evenly matched, how about we play for five bucks a hole?"

The first fellow says that he usually plays alone and really doesn't like to bet, but agrees to the terms.

The second guy wins the rest of the holes and as they're walking off the eighteenth green, and while counting his $80, he confesses that he's the pro at a neighboring course and likes to pick on suckers.

The first guy then reveals that he's the Parish Priest at the local Catholic Church to which the pro gets all flustered and apologetic and offers to give the priest back his money.

The Priest says, "No, no. You won fair and square and I was foolish enough to bet with you. You keep your winnings."

The pro asks, "Well, is there anything I can do to make it up to you?"

The Priest replies, "Well, you could come to Mass on Sunday and make a donation. Also, if you can bring your mother and father along, I'll marry them for you."

Generous Golfer

One day a golfer brought his regular golfing buddies together, and gave them each $50,000 cash and instructed them that upon his death, they were to throw it into the coffin, because he wanted to take it with him.

As luck would have it, he died soon after and when the funeral was over, his buddies met.

The doctor in the group said, "I have a confession to make. I put in an empty envelope and I used the money to buy equipment for the free clinic."

The priest said, "Me too, only I used the money to help build a youth center."

Somewhat shocked, the last member of the group, a lawyer, said, "I can't believe you guys went back on your word."

The others asked him if he actually put the $50,000 in the coffin.

He replied, "I most certainly did - I wrote him out a personal check for the full amount."

The Dead Parrot

At dawn the telephone rings.

"Hello, Senor Branston? This is Ernesto the caretaker at your country house."

"Ah yes, Ernesto. What can I do for you? Is there a problem?"

"I am just calling to advise you, Senor, that your parrot died"

"My parrot? Dead? My multiple prize winning parrot?"

"Si, Senor, that's the one."

"Damn! That's a real shame. I spent a fortune on that bird."

"What did he die from?"

"From eating rotten meat, Senor"

"Rotten meat? Who the hell fed him rotten meat?"

"Nobody, Senor. He ate the meat of the dead horse."

"What dead horse?"

"Your thoroughbred, Senor. He died from all that work pulling the water cart."

"What water cart?"

"The one we used to put out the fire, Senor."

"What fire?"

"The one at your house, Senor. A candle fell and the curtains caught on fire."

"What the f*ck? There's electricity at the house. What was the candle for?"

"For the funeral, Senor."

"What funeral?"

"Your wife's, Senor. She showed up one night out of the blue and I thought she was a burglar. So I hit her with your new PXG Tungsten Echo Plus Driver."

"Ernesto, if you broke that driver, you're in deep sh*t."

Tough Round

A man comes home after a terrible round of golf.

He plops down on the couch in front of the television, and tells his wife, "Get me a beer before it starts."

The wife sighs and gets him a beer. Ten minutes later, he says, "Get me another beer before it starts."

She looks annoyed, but fetches another beer and puts it down next to him.

He finishes that beer and a few minutes later says, "Get me another beer, it's going to start any minute."

The wife is furious. She yells at him, "You've been out golfing all day. Is that all you're going to do tonight? Drink beer and sit in front of that TV? You're nothing but a lazy, drunken, fat slob, and furthermore . . ."

The man sighs and says, "And now it's started."

The Witty Golfer

After a particularly poor round of golf, Pete skipped the 19th hole and was walking towards his car when a policeman stopped him and asked, "Did you tee off on the sixteenth hole about twenty minutes ago?"

"Yes," Pete responded.

"Did you happen to hook your ball so that it went over the trees and off the course?"

"Yes, I did. How did you know?" he asked.

"Well," said the policeman, "Your ball flew out onto the road and crashed through a driver's windshield. The car went out of control and crashed into a fire truck."

The policeman continued, "The fire truck couldn't make it to the fire, and the building burned down. All that because you hooked a tee shot. So, what are you going to do about it?"

Pete replied, "I think I'll close my stance a little bit, tighten my grip and lower my right thumb."

Heart Attack

A husband and wife are on the eighth green when suddenly she collapses from a heart attack.

"Help me dear," she groans to her husband.

The husband ran off saying, "I'll go and get some help."

A little while later he returned, picked up his putter and began to line up his putt.

His wife raises her head off the green, glares at him and says, "I'm dying here and you're putting?"

"Don't worry dear," says the husband calmly, "I found a cardiologist on the fourth hole and he's on his way to help you."

"How long will it take for him to arrive?" she weakly asks.

"Not long, darling," says her husband. "Everybody has already agreed to let him play through."

The Lord of Great Darkness

The devil was having a meeting with the junior demons.

He stood up and said, "You useless lot of sissies, there is far too much good in the world. You are here in hell to help make a man's life a misery. Instead you waste your time playing silly games. I want to know what you are going to do about it."

Just then a small devil who was new to the job nervously said, "Oh, Lord of great darkness. I know I am nowhere near as powerful as you but can I make a suggestion? It seems to me that if we could build them up and knock them down, the pain would be so great that we will soon gain control."

Just as he said that a more experienced demon said, "Are you suggesting golf?"

The devil himself interrupted and said, "No. We don't want to finish them off that quickly."

The Leprechaun

One fine day in Ireland, a guy is out golfing and on the 12th hole he slices his drive into the woods on the side of the fairway.

He goes looking for his ball and comes across this little guy lying on the ground with a huge lump on his head, and the golf ball right beside him.

"Goodness," says the golfer, and proceeds to revive the poor little guy.

Upon awaking, the little guy says, "Well, you caught me fair and square. I am a leprechaun and I will grant you three wishes."

The golfer says, "I can't take anything from you, I'm just glad I didn't hurt you too badly," and he continues his round of golf.

Watching the golfer walk away, the leprechaun thinks to himself, "He was a nice enough guy, and he did catch me, so I will have to do something for him in return. I'll give him the three things that I would want. I'll give him unlimited money, a great golf game, and a great sex life."

Well, a year later the same golfer hits one into the same woods on the same hole and goes off looking for his ball.

When he finds the ball he sees the same leprechaun and asks how he is doing. The leprechaun says, "I'm fine, and might I ask how your golf game is?"

The golfer says, "It's incredible these days. I play to par every time."

The leprechaun says, "I did that for you. And might I ask how your money is holding out?"

The golfer says, "Well, now that you mention it, every time I put my hand in my pocket, I pull out a ten Euros note."

The leprechaun smiles and says, "I did that for you. And might I ask how your sex life is?"

The golfer looks at him a little shyly and says, "Well, maybe once or twice a week."

The leprechaun stammers, "Once or twice a week?"

The golfer, a little embarrassed, looks at him and says, "Well, that's not too bad for a Catholic priest in a small parish."

The Hospital Visit

A man staggered into a hospital with concussion, multiple bruises, a black eye, and a five iron wrapped tightly around his throat.

The doctor asked him, "What happened to you?"

The bruised guy replied, "Well, I was playing a round of golf with my wife, when at a difficult hole, she sliced her ball into a cow pasture. We went to look for it and while I was looking around I noticed one of the cows had something white at its rear end."

He continued, "I walked over, lifted its tail, and sure enough, there was a golf ball with my wife's monogram on it - stuck right in the middle of the cow's butt."

"I held the cow's tail up and I yelled to my wife, 'Hey Honey, this looks like yours.'"

"I don't remember much after that."

Arnie, Jack and Tiger

Arnold Palmer, Jack Nicklaus and Tiger Woods are standing at the throne of heaven.

God looks at the three of them and says, "Before granting you a place at my side, I must ask you what you have learned in life and what you believe in."

God asks Arnie, "What do you believe?"

Arnie thinks long and hard, looks God in the eye, and says, "I believe in hard work, and in staying true to family and friends. I believe in giving. I was lucky, but I always tried to do right by my army of fans."

God can't help but see the essential goodness of Palmer, and offers him a seat to his left.

God asks Nicklaus, "What do you believe?"

Jack says, "I believe passion, discipline, courage and honor are the fundamentals of life. I, too, have been lucky, but win or lose; I've always tried to be a true sportsman, both on and off the golf course."

God is greatly moved by Jack's eloquence, and he offers him a seat to his right.

God turns to Woods and says, "And you, Tiger, what do you believe?"

Tiger replies, "I believe you're in my seat."

Hitting Over A Tree

A young man with a few hours to spare one afternoon figures that if he hurries and plays quickly, he can get in nine holes before he has to head home.

As he is about to tee off, an old guy asks if he can join him.

Although worried this will slow him down, the younger man says, "Of course."

To his surprise, the old man plays speedily. He doesn't hit the ball very far, but it goes straight.

When they reach the 9th fairway, the young man is facing a tough shot. A large pine tree is in front of his ball, directly between it and the green.

After a little time pondering how to hit the shot, the old man says, "You know, when I was your age, I'd hit the ball right over that tree."

With the gauntlet thrown down, and a challenge before him, the young man swings hard, hits the ball, watches it fly into the branches, rattle around, and land at the base of the tree.

"Of course," says the old man, "when I was your age, that tree was only three feet tall."

Gotcha

Ronnie was a 9 handicapper, and one day he challenged the pro to a match off scratch. He proposed they put up $100 each on the outcome.

"But," Ronnie said to the pro, "since you're so much better than me, you have to give me three 'gotchas'."

"A 'gotcha'?" the golf pro asked, "what's that?"

"Don't worry," Ronnie replied, "I'll use one of my 'gotchas' on the first tee and you'll understand."

The golf pro figured that whatever 'gotchas' were, giving up only three of them was no big deal - especially if one had to be used on the first tee. So he agreed to the bet, and the pro and Ronnie headed to the first tee to start their match.

Later in the bar, club members were amazed to see the pro handing Ronnie $100. The pro had lost to Ronnie and they asked the pro what happened.

"Well," the pro said, "I took the club back on the first tee, and as I started my downswing, Ronnie knelt behind me, reached up between my legs and grabbed my crotch, and yelled 'Gotcha.'"

A Liar and a Cheater

Jeremy and Barry are on the first tee when Jeremy says, "Let's play for $5."

Barry agrees, and they start their rounds.

It's a close match, and the two friends reach the 17th hole with Barry ahead by one stroke. After Jeremy hits a great drive, right down the middle, Barry steps up and promptly hooks a ball into the deep rough and trees.

Barry says to Jeremy, "Help me find my ball. I'll look in this patch of trees, and you look around over there."

They look and look, but no ball can be found. The three-minute time limit on searching for lost balls is about to run out and Barry gets desperate. He gives a quick glance over to Jeremy to see if he is looking, then swiftly reaches into his pocket and drops a new ball into the rough.

"I've found my ball." Barry shouts out triumphantly.

Jeremy looks over with great disappointment.

"After all the years we've been friends," Jeremy says, "you'd cheat me at golf for a measly five bucks?"

"What do you mean cheat?" Barry asks indignantly. "I found my ball right here."

Jeremy lets out a heavy sigh. "And you'd lie to me, too? All for a tiny amount of money? You'd cheat me and lie to me, for what? For five bucks? I can't believe you'd stoop so low."

"Well what makes you so sure I'm cheating and lying, anyway?" Barry asks.

"Because," Jeremy replies, "I've been standing on your ball for the last three minutes."

The Deaf Mute

A guy about to tee off was approached by a man who held out a card that read, "I am a deaf mute. May I please play through?"

The first man gave the card back, angrily shaking his head, and saying, "No, you CANNOT play through."

He assumed the guy was able to lip read so he mouthed, "I can't believe you would try to use your handicap to your own advantage like that. Shame on you."

The deaf man walked away and the first man hit his ball onto the green and then walked off to finish the hole.

Just as he was about to putt the ball he was hit in the head with a golf ball that knocked him out cold.

When he came to a few minutes later, he looked around and saw the deaf mute sternly looking at him, one hand on his hip, the other hand holding up four fingers.

Baptist Pastor

A Baptist pastor decides to skip his sermon on a Sunday so that he can play golf instead. He's out on the course on his own when an angel asks God, "Are you going to allow this pastor to do this rather than be at church?"

God says, "Watch this."

The pastor hit a 325 yard tee shot at the next hole, the ball took an incredibly friendly onward bounce and the ball ran into the hole for a hole in one.

The angel was astonished and asked, "Why did you reward him? I was expecting you to punish him."

God smiled and replied, "Think about it. Who is he going to tell?"

Health Food

An 85 years-old couple, having been married almost 60 years, die tragically in a car crash. They have been in good health the last ten years, mainly due to the wife's neurotic interest in health food.

When they reached the Pearly Gates, St. Peter took them to their mansion, which was decked out with a beautiful kitchen and master bath suite, complete with Jacuzzi. As they 'oohed and aahed' the old man asked St. Peter how much this was going to cost.

"It's free," St. Peter replied, "This is Heaven."

Next they went to see the championship golf course the home backed up to. They would have golfing privileges every day, and each week the course changed to a new one representing the greatest golf courses on Earth.

The old man asked, "What are the green fees?"

"This is Heaven," St. Peter replied. "It's free."

Next they went to the clubhouse and saw the lavish buffet lunch with the cuisines of the world laid out.

"Where are the low-fat and low-cholesterol foods?" the old man asked.

St. Peter replied, "You can eat as much as you like of whatever you like and never get fat and you never get sick. This is Heaven."

The old man glared at his wife and said, "You and your #@%&~ bran muffins. I could have been here ten years ago!"

The Incredible Golf Ball

Two friends were about to tee off when one fellow noticed that his partner had only one golf ball.

"Don't you have at least one other golf ball?" he asked.

The other guy replied that he only needed one.

"Are you sure?" the friend persisted. "What happens if you lose that ball?"

The other guy replied, "This is a very special golf ball. I won't lose it so I don't need another one."

"Well," the friend asked, "what happens if you mis-hit your shot and the ball goes into a lake?"

"That's okay," he replied, "this special golf ball floats. I'll be able to retrieve it."

"Well, what happens if you hit it into the trees and it gets lost among the bushes and shrubs?"

The other guy replied, "That's okay too. You see, this special golf ball has a homing beacon. I'll be able to get it back - no problem."

Exasperated, the friend asks, "Okay. Let's say our game goes late, the sun goes down, and you hit your ball into a sand trap. What are you going to do then?"

No problem," says the other guy, "you see, this ball is fluorescent. I'll be able to see it in the dark."

Impressed, the friend asks, "Where did you get a golf ball like that anyway?"

The other guy replies, "I found it."

Unlucky Golfer

Lady Luck was seldom kind to Sam. Although Sam had a real zest for life he was constantly beset by bad luck.

He loved poker but poker did not love him; he played the stock market but always seemed to be the one who bought high and sold low.

His life seemed to be full of more downs than ups.

His greatest delight was his golf game. Not that Sam was a great golfer; in fact, he rarely managed to break 100.

Finally Sam became ill and passed away. But just before he died, he asked that his remains be cremated and his ashes be scattered on the fairway on the ninth hole of his home course.

Accordingly, a gathering assembled to carry out Sam's wishes. It was a bright sunny day and was going well. Then, as the ashes were being strewn, a gust of wind came up and blew poor old Sam out of bounds.

Failing Eyesight

Jimmy was an avid golfer his entire life.

As he got into his seventies, his eyes started to fail him. His eyesight had gotten so bad, that he couldn't find his ball once he'd hit it.

He didn't want to give the game up, so he went to see the family eye doctor.

The doctor said there wasn't much he could do, but he knew of a 93 years old man named Alfred who still had perfect sight, in fact he could see like an eagle.

The doctor gave Jimmy the old man's name and suggested that he could use him to watch where he hit his golf ball.

Jimmy, of course, was doubtful but he made arrangements to bring Alfred along.

On the first tee, Jimmy drove his ball about 200 yards, but of course, he couldn't see where it went.

Jimmy asked Alfred, "Did you see my drive?"

Alfred replied, "I sure did. That was a beautiful shot."

Jimmy excitedly asked, "Where did it go?"

Alfred replied, "Hmmm. I forget."

Double Trouble

Terry had just completed a rough divorce and decided he would like to play a relaxing round of golf.

While waiting on the first tee, he reached into the trash can and pulled out a rusty lamp. He rubbed it to get the dirt off and a genie popped out. The genie told the guy that he would grant him three wishes, with the condition that his ex-wife would get double what he wished for.

Terry said he wanted a Lamborghini. The genie reminded him that his ex-wife would get two of them. The guy had no hesitation and said he didn't care if his ex-wife had two, as long as he had one for himself. Poof! The genie said it was done.

His next wish was $1 million in the back of his Lamborghini. The genie reminded him that his wife would receive $2 million. The guy said he didn't care and told the genie to fulfill his wish. Poof! The genie said it was done.

For Terry's final wish, he thought long and hard. He handed the genie his 6-iron and said calmly, "Beat me half to death."

The Mermaid

A Frenchman, an Italian and a Scotsman were playing golf on a links course when they spotted a stunning mermaid on the shore.

They all dropped their clubs and ran down for a closer look. The mermaid was incredibly beautiful and voluptuous.

The Frenchman, burning with desire, said, "Have you ever been kissed?" "No, I haven't," answered the mermaid. So the Frenchman walked over and kissed her deeply and slowly. "Hmmm," sighed the mermaid, "that's nice."

The Italian, not to be outdone, asked the mermaid, "Have you ever been fondled?" "No, I haven't," whispered the mermaid. So the Italian walked over and hugged and fondled her warmly. The mermaid sighed, "Hmmm, that's nice."

Finally the Scotsman asked her, "Have you ever been screwed?" "No, I haven't," answered the mermaid. "Well, you have now," said the Scotsman, "'because the tide's out!"

Lightning Strike

Ian and his buddy were trying desperately to get in 18 holes before the predicted thunder and lightning arrived.

Although rushing, he was playing the best round of his life, and decided to stay on the course although the weather grew worse.

He hooked his drive into the trees on the 15th hole as the storm came in.

He found his ball in a bad lie and decided to just play back onto the fairway. However, as he took his club to the top of his backswing, lightning struck down from the sky catching his steel shafted 9 iron.

His friend hurried over only to see a crater in the ground and no sign of Ian or his clubs - he was gone.

When he reached the Pearly Gates, Saint Peter said, "We are so sorry to have taken you at such an early age, however, as you love the game so much, and you had the round of your life going, we decided to bring your clubs along with you so that you can play all the courses of heaven which are more incredible than any golf course that you have ever played."

The man started crying, to which Saint Peter said, "I know, you have left behind many loved ones."

Ian said, "No, that's not it."

Saint Peter said, "Yes my son, you also had an unbelievable life and a great career."

"No, that's not it either," sobbed Ian.

Saint Peter said, "Well then, what could make you so unhappy, that you would cry so much?"

Ian looked up as the tears flooded from his eyes and replied, "I think I left my wedge next to the 14th green."

Play The Ball Where It Lies

Two old friends, Neil and Maurice, were playing golf one day.

Neil was a stickler for the rules and always insisted that they adhere strictly to the rule about not improving a lie.

After a few holes, Maurice's ball landed on a cart path.

As he reached down to pick up his ball to get relief Neil said, "You cannot do that – you cannot improve your lie."

No matter how much Maurice tried to explain that he was entitled to free relief, Neil would simply not allow it.

So Maurice went to the cart to get a club.

He stood over the ball and took a few practice swings, each time scraping the club on the cart path, sending out lots of sparks.

Finally, after several practice swings he took his shot. The ball took off and landed on the green about ten feet from the pin.

"Great shot," Neil exclaimed. "What club did you use?"

"YOUR 7 iron." Maurice replied.

Damn it – I Missed

A priest and an atheist are playing a round of golf.

On the first hole the atheist misses a short putt and exclaims, "Dammit, I missed."

The priest tells him, "Don't use that kind of language or God will punish you."

On the second hole, the atheist tries to chip onto the green and instead lands in a sand bunker, and he bellows, "Dammit I missed."

The priest once again issued a warning to him about God punishing those who curse.

The round carries on in much the same way, with the atheist continuing to cry "Dammit I missed." every time he hits an errant ball and the priest continues to admonish him about God's wrath.

Finally, they get to the eighteenth hole and the score is tied. The atheist needs to make a four feet putt in order to win. Again he misses, and again, he curses, "Dammit I missed."

This time, before the priest can respond, the clouds in the sky open up, and a bolt of lightning shoots down and hits the priest; there is a large puff of smoke, and there lies the priest, dead.

Then, from the clouds above comes a deep voice booming, "Dammit, I missed."

Ship High In Transit

In the 17th century, most products were transported by ship and it was also before the invention of commercial fertilizer, so large shipments of manure were common.

It was shipped dry, because it weighed less but once water hit it, fermentation began which produced methane gas as a by-product.

The manure was stored in bundles below deck and once wet with sea water, methane began to build up.

If someone came below decks at night with a lantern, then Boom, there would often be a huge explosion.

Several ships were destroyed in this manner before the cause of the explosions was determined.

Afterwards, the bundles of manure were stamped with the term "Ship High In Transit" which directed the crew to stow it in the upper decks so that any water that came into the hold would not reach this volatile cargo and produce the explosive gas.

Thus evolved the term "S.H.I.T" (**S**hip **H**igh **I**n **T**ransit) which has come down through the centuries and is still in use today.

You probably did not know the true history of this word.

Neither did I. I always thought it was a golf term.

The Lost City

For months the archaeologists had been toiling deep in the jungle, clearing creepers and choking undergrowth from the faint traces of a Lost City.

Their excitement mounted as the site's extraordinary purpose became evident. Wide avenues of giant cobblestones had small circular holes every few hundred yards.

It simply had to be...a golf course!

Any doubt was dispelled by the discovery of sculptures and paintings of human figures using primitive prototypes of golf clubs.

The next step was to interrogate the local tribesmen about the traditions associated with the prehistoric golf club of the Lost City. It was soon learned that the tribal leaders did indeed have legends of the Old Ones who followed a weekly ritual using primitive clubs and balls, until they were overcome by tragedy.

Via an interpreter, a professor asked, "If only we knew why they gave up golf, making it vanish for centuries before rediscovery."

The tribal elder, surprised, made a sweeping gesture and replied.

"Simple," was the translation, "they could not afford the green fees."

The Ducks

Three golfing buddies died in a car crash and went to heaven.

Upon arrival, they saw the most beautiful golf course they have ever seen. St. Peter told them they were welcome to play the course, but he cautioned them, "Don't step on the ducks."

The men had blank expressions on their faces, and one of them said, "The ducks?"

"Yes," St. Peter said. "There are millions of ducks walking around the golf course, and when one of them is stepped on, he squawks, and then the one next to him squawks, and soon they're all making a dreadful racket, and it really breaks the tranquility. If you step on the ducks, you'll be severely punished."

The men start playing the course, and within 30 minutes, one of the guys stepped on a duck. The duck squawked, and soon there was a cacophony of noise with countless ducks quacking.

St. Peter then appeared with an ugly woman and asked, "Who stepped on a duck?"

"I did," admitted one of the men.

St. Peter immediately pulled out a pair of handcuffs and cuffed the man to the plain woman. "I told you not to step on the ducks," he said. "Now you'll be handcuffed together for eternity."

The two other men were very cautious not to step on any ducks, but a couple of weeks later, one of them accidentally did. The quacks were as deafening as before, and within minutes, St. Peter walked up with a woman who was even uglier than the other one. He determined who stepped on the duck by seeing the fear in the man's face, and he cuffed him to the woman.

"I told you not to step on the ducks," St. Peter said. "Now you'll be handcuffed together for eternity."

The third man was now extra careful. Some days he wouldn't even move for fear of nudging a duck. After three months of this, he still hadn't stepped on a duck.

Then, out of the blue, St. Peter walked up to the man with the most beautiful woman the man had ever seen. St. Peter smiled and without a word, handcuffed him to the beautiful woman and walked off.

The man, knowing that he would be handcuffed to this woman for eternity, let out a sigh and said, "What have I done to deserve this?"

The woman replied, "I don't know about you, but I stepped on a duck."

Slow Group

The same group of golfers played every Wednesday afternoon at 1pm. They were known as the WAG Society and they always finished their rounds by 4:30pm so they could enjoy a bottle or two of wine.

One Wednesday, they ran into a four-ball ahead of them, who were playing incredibly slowly. The guys in the WAG Society waved at the group in front many times, but the group ahead never moved aside to let them through.

After a frustrating almost five hours round, the WAG members came into the bar fuming. The slow group was at a table across the room and the whole bar could hear the swearing coming from the WAGs.

Finally, a waitress approached the WAGs and said, "You guys should lighten up. That group you're cursing? They can't see. They're blind golfers and I think it's great they can even play."

One of the group felt terrible and told the others, "The waitress is right. Tell you what, we should send them over a bottle of Rioja on our tab."

Another one in the group said, "That's a good idea, but let's send them a bottle of Malbec instead."

Everyone looked at the leader of the group for him to approve.

"Sod them," he grumbled, "Tell those idiots to play at night."

Here is an alternative religious version of the gag.

Two pastors, one Catholic and one Protestant, and a Jewish rabbi were playing together.

The group ahead of them were playing very slowly and weren't gesturing for a play-through.

After several holes of this agonizingly slow golf the three clerics began to get very impatient, each muttering their own curses upon the group ahead of them.

Soon the Marshall came by, and he was called over by the holy men who told him, "We're sick of being held-up by these guys ahead of us who won't allow us to play through."

The Marshall said, "I'm sorry, gentlemen, but those men are both deaf and blind."

The Protestant wailed, "Jesus, please forgive me for my bad thoughts and blaspheming these poor souls."

The Catholic cried, "Oh please forgive me, Mary, for my bad thoughts and blaspheming these poor souls."

The rabbi exclaimed, "So why can't they play at night?"

How Many?

John and Adrian were two of the bitterest rivals at the club. Neither man trusted the other's arithmetic.

One day they were playing a heated match and watching each other like hawks.

After holing out on the fourteenth green and marking his six on the scorecard, John asked Adrian, "What did you have?"

Adrian went through the motions of mentally counting up his shots.

"Six," he exclaimed and then hastily corrected himself. "No, no....a five."

Calmly John marked the scorecard, saying out loud "Eight."

"Eight?" Adrian said, "I couldn't possibly have had eight."

John said, "Well, you claimed six, then changed it to five, but you actually had seven."

"Then why did you mark down eight?" asked Adrian.

John told him, "I am giving you a one stroke penalty, for improving your lie."

A Good Golfer

Dick brings a friend to play golf with two of his regular golf buddies.

His buddies asked him if his new friend can play golf and Dick replied, "He's very good."

The new guy hits his first tee shot into the bush, and his buddies looked at Dick and said, "We thought you said your friend was a good golfer."

Dick replied, "Just watch, he will recover."

They then saw the ball fly out of the bush onto the green where the new guy takes two putts and makes his par.

On the second hole, he hits the ball into the lake. The two buddies look at Dick again and said, "You said this guy was good."

Dick replied, "Just watch, he will recover."

The new guy walked into the lake.

Two minutes pass and there's no sign of him.

Suddenly, an outstretched hand comes out of the water and Dick's buddies tell him to dive in to save his drowning friend.

Dick replied, "You don't understand, that just means he wants a 5 iron."

Hole In One

Paul had been playing golf for over twenty years but never had a hole-in-one.

As he was hacking away in a bunker he voiced the thought, "I'd give anything to get a hole-in-one."

"Would you give up half your sex life?" came a voice from behind.

Startled, Paul turned around to see a small grinning, red-clad figure with horns and a tail.

"Yes, Yes I would." Paul replied.

"It's a deal then." said the horned figure who then disappeared.

On the very next hole Paul's tee shot looked good the moment he hit it, with the ball flying into the hole for his first ever hole-in-one.

Paul was the happiest he had ever been on a golf course, and as he was screaming with joy, he noticed that the little horned figure in red had re-appeared and was standing beside him on the tee-box.

"Now for our bargain," the horned figure said. "You remember you must give up half your sex life."

Paul frowned and said, "Yes I do, but that gives me a bit of a problem."

"Don't try and back out of this," cried the figure. "We struck a bargain and you agreed to it."

Paul replied, "Yes, of course. But I have a problem. Which half of my sex life do you want - the thinking or the dreaming?"

Behind A Tree

Two English guys were playing golf when the first one said, "I really need to take a crap."

The second guy replied, "Well go behind that tree and do your stuff."

The first guy looks over at the tree and says, "But I don't have any toilet paper."

The second man remarks, "You have five pounds on you, don't you? Just use it to wipe yourself."

Reluctantly, the first guy goes and does his stuff.

Minutes later he comes back with crap all over him.

The second guy asks, "Damn, what happened? Didn't you use the five pounds?"

The first guy replies, "Yes, but have you ever tried to wipe your @rse with four pound coins and two 50 pences?"

The Genie In The Bottle

A young married couple are playing golf, when the wife has a wild tee shot, which sails off into a nearby villa, breaking a window pane.

The young couple approach the house with caution and are amazed at how beautiful it is.

Their curiosity gets the better of them and they decide to knock on the door.

Hearing no answer and noticing the door is open, they elect to go in.

Entering the beautiful home they notice a golf ball and an ancient broken bottle near the broken window.

Out of the blue a distinguished middle-aged gentleman introduces himself to them saying, "Thank you for freeing me. I have been trapped in that bottle for five thousand years, and now I can grant three wishes for releasing me: I will grant you one wish each, but the third is up to me.

The husband without even thinking about it says, "I want a Ferrari."

His wife then says, "I want a wardrobe full of designer dresses."

They hear the reply, "So be it! My desire is to have sex with the lady present. After five thousand years of abstinence, I hope you will understand."

The husband and wife agree since their extravagant wishes had been granted.

So the wife goes upstairs for a lengthy sex session.

Lying in bed afterwards, the man turns to the woman and asks, "How old are you and your husband?"

She replies breathlessly, "We're both twenty nine, but why do you ask?"

He says, "Well, you would think by now you would have stopped believing in genies."

Imaginary Balls

Two golfers join up at the first tee and each explains that due to a psychological problem, they play slightly differently than most golfers.

They soon learn that they both have the same doctor who has prescribed a game of golf using an imaginary golf ball to reduce stress. And so they tee off with their imaginary balls.

After a day of splitting fairways and getting many pars and birdies, they reach the 18th hole. The first one tees off with his imaginary ball.

He says, "Look at that, a beautiful shot which has finished just on the edge of the green."

The second guy hits his imaginary ball and indicates that it has also landed on the edge of the green, and next to the other ball.

They get to the green and the first guy lines up the putt and drains his 20-footer to the bottom of the cup.

He says, "You wouldn't believe it, my ball rolled into the cup, I win."

The second guy responds, "You won't believe it either, you just hit my ball by mistake. You forfeit the hole, and the match."

Mind The Gap

Gordon and his friend Tom were playing a round of golf with their wives

Gordon hooked his drive on the 5th hole, and when he found his ball, it was right up against the greenkeeper's buildings. His wife advised him to hit the shot through a narrow gap between the side of the building and some branches.

"I can't do that," Gordon said. "Look how narrow that gap is."

His wife was persistent in urging him on, and she persuaded Gordon to attempt the risky shot.

So, Gordon took a mighty swing and struck the ball and watched it bounce off a tree branch and hit his wife in the head, knocking her stone cold dead.

A week after the funeral, Gordon was back on the course, this time with his friend, Ashley. Gordon teed up the ball on the fifth tee and hit the exact shot he had hit a week before.

He found his ball in the same spot, and once again his partner advised him to hit through the gap.

"No way," Gordon said. "I can't hit that shot."

"Why not?" Ashley asked him.

"Well," Gordon replied, "you know what happened last time."

"No, I don't," said Ashley. "What happened?"

"Well, last time I tried that shot," Gordon said, "I made a double bogey."

Three Dogs

A doctor, an architect and a hot shot lawyer were dining at the country club one day, when the conversation turned to the subject of their dogs, as they apparently had astonishing talents. A large wager was placed on who had the most intelligent dog.

The physician called out for his dog first shouting, "Hippocrates, come." The dog ran in, and the doctor whispered something in his ear. Hippocrates ran out onto the golf course and dug for a while, producing a number of bones. He carried the bones back into the club and then assembled them into a human skeleton. The physician patted Hippocrates on the head, and gave him a cookie for being so clever.

The architect called for his dog, "Bauhaus, come." The dog ran in and was told to do his stuff. The dog proceeded to chew the skeleton to rubble, but re-assembled the fragments into a scale model of the Taj Mahal. The architect patted his dog for his efforts and gave him a cookie.

The attorney called for his dog, "Horseshit, come." The dog ran in and the attorney told him to do his stuff. Horseshit instantly f*cked the other two dogs, ate their cookies, auctioned the Taj Mahal replica to the other club members for his fee, and then went outside to watch his master play golf.

Four Sons

Four men were due to play golf, and three had arrived and while they were waiting on the fourth to show up they started discussing their children.

The first man told the others how his son had started out as a used car salesman, and he now owned a car dealership and was doing so well, that last year he gave a friend a brand new car as a gift.

The second man said that his son has his own construction firm having started work as a bricklayer's apprentice and that he's doing so well that last year he was able to give a good friend of his a brand-new house.

The third man boasted that his son has worked his way up through a stock trading company, and is now so successful that in the last month he gave a good friend a large amount of shares in IBM as a gift.

As the fourth man joins them, the other three guys inform him that they have been discussing how successful their respective sons are, and are curious to find out how his son is getting on.

He tells them, "Actually I'm not pleased with how my son has turned out. For many years he has been a hairdresser, and he recently announced to me that he is gay. However, looking on the bright side, he must be good at what he does, because his last three boyfriends have given him a car, a brand new house and some shares in IBM."

The Gorilla

Two men played golf together frequently. One had a higher handicapper than the other but he always refused to take any strokes to even up the game.

One Saturday morning, he shows up with a gorilla at the first tee.

He says to his friend, "I've been trying to beat you for so long that I'm about ready to give up. But, I heard about this golfing gorilla, and I was wondering if it would be alright if he plays for me today. In fact if you're game, I'd like to try to get back all the money I've lost to you this year. I figure that comes to about a thousand bucks. Are you willing?"

The other guy thought about it for a minute, and then decided to play the gorilla. "After all, just how could a gorilla be any good at golf?" he thought.

Well, the first hole was a straight long par 4 of 450 yards.

The guy hits a beautiful tee shot, 275 yards down the middle, leaving himself a 6 iron to the green. The gorilla takes a few powerful practice swings and then hits his ball 450 yards, right at the pin, stopping just two feet away from the hole.

The guy turns to his friend and says, "That's incredible, I would have never believed it if I hadn't seen it with my own eyes."

He continues, "You know what, I've seen enough. I've got no interest in being totally humiliated by this gorilla golfing machine. You send this frigging gorilla back to where-ever he comes from. I need a large stiff drink, and I'll write you a check."

After handing over the check, and well into his second double the guy asks, "By the way, how's that gorilla's putting?"

The other guy replies, "Same as his driving."

"That good, huh?"

The other guy replies, "No, I mean, he hits putts the same way - 450 yards, right down the middle!"

Loudspeaker Announcement

An elderly gentleman was addressing the ball when an announcement came over the loud-speaker, "Will the gentleman on hole number one please not hit from the Ladies' tee box."

The old gent backs away, a little distracted, then approaches his ball again. As he does, there is another announcement over the loud-speaker, "Will the gentleman on hole number one please not hit from the Ladies' tee box."

The old man is getting irritated now, and after backing away from his shot, approaches his ball one more time. This time the announcement came, "We need the gentleman on hole number one to move off the Ladies' tee box."

The old timer turns around and yells, "I need the announcer to shut up and let me play my second shot."

The Hooker

Martin is having a bad time of it and he keeps slicing the ball. It is so bad that he's embarrassed to be seen playing, and he decides that he'll play on his own early in the morning so that nobody can see him.

On the first hole he slices the ball savagely and it flies over the golf club fence.

Martin is so depressed he packs his clubs up and goes home.

The next day he decides to persevere and tries again. However, he slices the ball over the fence again but this time he sees the ball narrowly miss a man out walking his dog. The golfer rushes over to apologize.

"You were here and did the same thing yesterday weren't you?" the man asks the golfer.

"Yeah, I seem to have a major slice right now." Martin answers.

"Did you see where yesterday's ball ended up?" the dog owner asks.

"No," says the golfer.

The dog owner said, "Oh it bounced off a lamp-post onto the main road. It caused a car to skid into a mother pushing a pram. Both the mother and baby were killed instantly."

"That's terrible," exclaims Martin, "What do you think I should do?"

The dog owner replied, "You need to close your stance and drop your left shoulder."

Religious Golf

Jesus and Saint Peter are golfing.

St. Peter steps up to the first hole, a short par four, and he hits the ball long and straight, and it finishes just short of the green.

Jesus is up next and he slices his ball and it heads over the fence into traffic on an adjacent road. It bounces off a car, onto the roof of a house and into the rain gutter, down the drain spout and onto a lily pad at the edge of a lake. A frog jumps up and snatches the ball in his mouth. As he does, an eagle swoops down and grabs the frog in its talons. As the eagle flies over the green, the frog croaks and drops the ball into the hole.

Saint Peter looks at Jesus, exasperated.

"Are you going to play golf properly?" he asks "Or are you just going to muck around?"

The Riders

Four elderly guys went into the pro shop after playing 18 holes of golf.

The pro asked, "Did you guys have a good game today?"

The first old guy said, "Yes, I had two riders today."

The second old guy said, "I had the most riders ever. I had four."

The third old guy said, "I had five riders, the same as last time."

The last old guy said, "I beat my old record. I had seven riders today."

After they went into the locker room, another golfer who had heard the old guys talking about their game went to the pro and said, "I've been playing golf for a long time and thought I knew all the terminology of the game, but what's a rider?"

The pro replied, "A rider is when you hit the ball far enough to actually get in the golf cart and ride to go to it."

The Desert Island

One day an Irishman, who has been stranded on a desert island for ten years, looks out to sea and sees a strange dot on the horizon.

He thinks to himself, "I wonder what that can be."

As the speck begins to get closer to the shore, he rules out the possibilities of it being a small boat, then even a raft.

Eventually, a stunning beautiful woman wearing a wet suit and scuba gear emerges from the surf onto the beach.

She approaches the speechless castaway and asks, "How long has it been since you've had a cigarette?"

He answers, "Ten long years."

With that, she unzips a waterproof pocket on her left arm and she pulls out a packet of cigarettes.

He takes one, lights it, takes a long drag and pronounces, "Sweet Jesus. That is good."

She looks at him and asks, "How long has it been since you've tasted Irish Whiskey?"

Trembling, the Irishman replies, "Ten long years."

She then unzips a sleeve on her right arm, pulls out a hipflask and then passes it to him.

He opens the flask, takes a gulp and declares, "Faith and begorah. That is absolutely fantastic."

She then slowly unzips the long zipper that runs down the front of her wet suit, smiles seductively and asks, "How long has it been since you've played around?"

With tears in his eyes, the Irishman falls to his knees and weeps, "Holy Moses, don't tell me you've got a set of golf clubs in there."

Agony Aunt

Dear Deirdre,

I really need your advice. I have suspected for some time now that my wife has been cheating on me. My wife has been going out with "the girls" a lot recently and when I ask who they are, she always says, "Just some friends from work."

I try to stay awake to look out for her coming home, but I usually fall asleep. Anyway, I have never approached the subject with my wife. I think deep down I just didn't want to know the truth, but last night she went out again and I decided to check on her. Around midnight, I decided to hide in the garage behind my golf clubs so I could get a good view of when she arrived home from a night out with "the girls".

While crouching behind my clubs I noticed that the graphite shaft on my driver appeared to have a hairline crack right by the club head.

Is this something I can fix myself or should I take it back to the pro shop?

Signed,

Perplexed

Grizzly Or Brown Bear?

The Montana State Department of Fish and Wildlife is advising golfers to take extra precautions, and be on the alert for bears while playing on the local golf courses. They advise golfers to wear noise-producing devices such as little bells on their clothing to alert, but not to startle the bears unexpectedly. They also advise golfers to carry pepper spray in the case of an encounter with a bear.

They say that it's also a good idea to watch for signs of bear activity on the courses. They recommend that golfers should be educated so that they can recognize the difference between black bear and grizzly bear droppings.

Black bear droppings are smaller and contain remains of nuts, berries and possibly squirrel, rabbit or gopher fur.

Grizzly bear droppings have small bells, golf-gloves, sunglasses and other similar golf items in them and they usually smell like pepper spray.

Just Like Frank

A man walks out of a bar just as a taxi comes along.

He flags the taxi down, and gets in, and the cabbie says, "Perfect timing. You're just like Frank."

The passenger asks, "Who?"

The cabbie says, "Frank Wilkinson. He is a guy who does everything right. Like my coming along when you needed a cab. It would have happened like that to Frank every single time."

The passenger says, "Yes, but there are always a few clouds over everybody."

The cabbie says, "Not Frank. He was a terrific golfer. He could have won the US Open, The Masters, The PGA and The Open if he had wanted to."

He continues, "He sang like an opera baritone, danced like a Broadway star, could play the piano brilliantly, had a mind like a computer. He could remember everybody's birthday. He knew all about wine, which foods to order and he could fix anything. Not like me. I change a fuse, and the whole street blacks out."

The passenger states, "He sounds an incredible guy."

The cabbie says, "He always knew the quickest way to go in traffic and avoid traffic jams, not like me. I always seem to get stuck in them. He knew how to treat a woman and make her feel good. And he'd never answer her back even if she was in the wrong; and his clothing was always immaculate."

The passenger remarks, "He sounds an amazing fellow. How did you meet him?"

The cabbie replies, "Well, I never actually met Frank."

The passenger asks, "Then how do you know so much about him?"

The cabbie replies, "I married his goddamn widow."

Confession

This man goes to confession and says, "Forgive me father for I have sinned."

The priest asks if he would like to confess his sins and the man replies that he used the 'F-word' over the weekend.

The priest says, "Just say three Hail Marys and try to watch your language."

The man replies that he would like to confess as to why he said the 'F-word.'

The priest sighs and tells him to continue.

He says, "Well father I played golf on Sunday with my buddies instead of going to church."

The priest says, "And you got upset over that and swore?"

The man replied, "No, that wasn't why I swore. On the first tee I duck-hooked my drive left into the trees."

The priest said, "Is that when you swore?"

The man replied, "No, it wasn't. When I walked up the fairway, I noticed my ball got a lucky bounce and I had a clear shot to the green. However, before I could hit the ball, a squirrel ran by and grabbed my ball and scurried up a tree."

The priest asked, "Is that when you said the 'F-word'?"

The man replied, "No, because an eagle then flew by and picked up the squirrel in its talons and flew away."

The priest let out a breath and queried, "Is that when you swore?"

The man replied, "No, because the eagle flew over the green and the dying squirrel let go of my golf ball and it landed 6 inches from the hole."

The priest shrieked, "Don't tell me you missed the f*cking putt!"

Chapter 6: Rude Golfing Jokes

If you feel you will be offended by rude jokes, you'd best skip this chapter.

Let's start with - it's not the size of your club that counts, it's how many strokes you take.

A wife walked into the bedroom and found her husband in bed with his golf clubs.

Seeing the astonished look on her face, he calmly said, "Well, you said I had to choose."

Q: What is the similarity between four-putting and masturbation?

A: You're ashamed of what you have done but you know it will happen again.

Q: How can you tell which golfer is a womanizer?

A: He gets his balls cleaned regularly.

Q: What did the golfer say after performing yoga?

A: "Damn, my shaft is all bent."

Q: How do you know a golfer is cheating on his wife?

A: He puts his driver in the wrong bag.

Q: What do you do after a round on a hot sunny day?

A: Wash your balls.

Q: What do you call Jessica Alba joining you and your buddies for a round of golf?

A: A Fantastic Four-Some.

Q: What do you call a dumb blonde at a golf course?

A: The 19th hole.

Q: Why did the blonde golf pro cheat on his wife?

A: Because he thought he needed to play around every day.

Q: What is the difference between a lost golf ball and the G-spot?

A: A man will spend 3 minutes looking for a lost golf ball.

An Irish golfer drove his ball into his German neighbor's garden. He went to ask for his ball and the neighbor said, "Sorry, old German custom dictates that possession is nine tenths of the law."

The man replied, "Well mate, an old Irish custom is that we take it in turns to kick each other in the bollocks, me first, and the last man standing gets to keep the ball."

"OK," says the German.

The Irishman then kicks him in the balls as hard as he can and then says, "You can keep the ball, mate."

A recent study had some interesting conclusions on the weight of golfers at a well-known golf club.

This study indicated that single golfers are 'skinnier' than married ones.

The study's explanation for this result was interesting. It seems that the single golfer goes out and plays his round of golf, has a 'refreshment' at the 19th hole, goes home and goes to his refrigerator, finds nothing decent there and so he goes to bed.

The married golfer goes out and plays his round of golf, has a 'refreshment' at the 19th hole, goes home and goes to bed, finds nothing decent there, so he goes to his refrigerator.

A married couple played golf together every day.

One day the man and his wife were on the first tee of their local course. He was on the white tee and she was waiting in front of him by the ladies tee.

He teed off and caught the ball cleanly; but unfortunately, it hit his wife smack in the back of the head killing her instantly.

There was an inquest on the wife's death, and the coroner said it was clear how she died, in that she was killed by a golf ball, and that there was a perfect imprint of a Titleist 1 golf ball on the back of her head.

The husband said, "Yes, that was my ball."

The coroner then went on to say that he was a bit concerned to find a Titleist 3 ball inserted up the woman's backside, and could the husband throw some light on this?

The husband said, "Oh that must have been my provisional. I wondered where that ball went."

One day this woman went to her local golf pro, and told him she had developed a huge slice.

Day and night he worked with her for three months.

Now she's the biggest hooker in town.

A blonde is standing by the first tee waiting for her golf lesson from the pro.

A fourball is in the process of teeing off. The first golfer addresses the ball and swings, hitting it 200 yards straight down the middle of the fairway.

"That was a good shot," said the blonde. "Not bad considering my impediment," said the golfer. "What's wrong with you?" said the blonde. "I have a glass eye," said the golfer. "I don't believe you, show me," said the blonde. He popped his eye out and showed her.

The next golfer addresses the ball and swings, hitting it 210 yards straight down the middle of the fairway. "That was a good shot," said the blonde. "Not bad considering my impediment," said the golfer. "What's wrong with you?" said the blonde. "I have a prosthetic arm," said the golfer. "I don't believe you, show me," said the blonde, so he screwed his arm off and showed her.

The next golfer addresses the ball and swings, hitting it 220 yards straight down the middle of the fairway. "That was a good shot," said the blonde. "Not bad considering my impediment," said the golfer. "What's wrong with you?" said the blonde. "I have a prosthetic leg," said the golfer. "I don't believe you, show me," said the blonde, so he screwed his leg off and showed her.

The fourth golfer addresses the ball and swings, hitting it 230 yards straight down the middle of the fairway. "That was a good shot," said the blonde. "Not bad considering my impediment," said the golfer. "What's wrong with you?" said the blonde. "I have an artificial heart," said the golfer. "I don't believe you, show me," said the blonde.

"I can't show you out here in the open," said the golfer. "Let's go behind the Pro Shop."

As the pair had not returned after five minutes, his golfing buddies decided to go and see what was holding their buddy up.

As they looked behind the Pro Shop, sure enough, there he was, screwing his heart out.

There was this guy who went golfing every Saturday and Sunday, it didn't matter what kind of weather – he played every weekend.

One Saturday he left the house early and headed for the golf course, but it was so bitterly cold that he decided he wouldn't golf that day and went back home.

His wife was still in bed when he got there, so he took off his clothes and snuggled up to her and said, "Terrible weather out there."

She replied, "Yeah, and can you believe my stupid husband went golfing."

Whilst out on the course, two work colleagues were discussing the hot new office manager at their company.

Lucas said, "I went back to her place last weekend and we had some great sex. She is much better in bed than my wife."

James said, "I went back to her place two days ago, and we had sex as well, but I still think your wife is better in bed."

A couple are playing in the annual Husband & Wife Club Championship. They are playing in a play-off hole and it is down to a 6 inch putt that the wife has to make.

Unfortunately, she misses the putt and they lose the match.

On the way home in the car the husband is fuming, and he says to his wife, "I can't believe that you missed that putt. That putt was no longer than my 'willy'."

The wife looked at her husband, smiled and said, "Yes dear, but it was much harder!"

At a cocktail party a guy sees a very attractive woman standing alone, so he approaches her, and says, "Hello and just who are you?"

She smiled seductively and said, "Hello to you. My name is Carmen."

"That's a beautiful name," he replied. "Is it a family name?"

"No," she replied. "As a matter of fact I gave the name to myself. It represents the things that I enjoy the most in life – cars and men. Therefore I chose 'Carmen.'"

"What's your name?" she asked.

He answered, "B. J. Boobsengolf."

An American guy travels to Tokyo on business.

One night, he's feeling a little frisky. He goes to a geisha bar. After a few more drinks, he hires one of the women to go back to his hotel for some action.

They begin to fool around, and eventually end up in bed. As they start to have sex, she begins moaning, then screaming. As she catches her breath, she begins shouting, "Machigatta ana! Machigatta ana!"

The guy doesn't speak any Japanese, but he is really enjoying it, and speeds up a bit as she keeps screaming, "Machigatta ana! Machigatta ana!"

After they are done, he pays her, and she leaves, barely able to walk out of the room.

The next day, he is playing golf with an executive at the Japanese company he had been meeting with.

Incredibly, he manages a hole in one.

He doesn't know any Japanese so he yells, "Machigatta ana! Machigatta ana!"

The Japanese guy he is playing with asks him, "What do you mean, wrong hole?"

Gary and Andrew are being held up by two women who are playing terribly slowly.

Finally, after watching the women in the distance as they stood over their putts for what seemed like an eternity, Andrew decided to do something.

"I'll walk ahead and ask them if we can play through," Andrew said.

He set off down the fairway, walking towards the women. But when he got halfway, he stopped, turned around and headed back to where Gary waited.

"I can't do it," Andrew said, sounding embarrassed. "One of them is my wife and the other is my mistress."

"OK," Gary said, "I'll go and ask them then."

Gary started up the fairway, only to stop halfway and turn back.

"What's wrong?" Andrew asked when Gary returned.

Gary replied, "Small world, isn't it?"

Bill is waiting to tee off for the start of his round when he sees Mark just finishing his round.

Bill notices that Mark is wet all over the front of his trousers and he asks how he got so wet. Mark tells him today was the first time he had played with bifocals. All day long, he could see two sizes for everything. There was a big club and a little club; a big ball and a little ball; etc.

Mark said that he hit the little ball with the big club and it went straight and long all day long. On the green, he putted the little ball into the big hole. He said that he played some of the best golf of his life.

Bill said, "I get that, but how did you get all wet?"

"Well," said Mark, "when I got to the 16th, I needed to urinate. I went into the woods and unzipped my fly. When I looked down, there were two of them; a big one and a little one. Well, I knew the big one wasn't mine, so I put it back in my pants."

A married man was having an affair with his secretary. One day, their passions overcame them and they went to her house for some afternoon delight.

Exhausted from the afternoon's activities, they fell asleep and awoke at around 7 p.m.

As the man put on his clothes, he told his secretary to take his shoes outside and rub them through the grass and dirt.

Mystified, she nonetheless complied and he slipped into his shoes and drove home.

"Where have you been?" demanded his wife when he entered the house.

"Darling," replied the man, "I can't lie to you. I've been having an affair with my secretary. I fell asleep in her bed and didn't wake up until seven o'clock."

The wife glanced down at his shoes and said, "You liar. You've been out playing golf."

Two women were playing golf. One teed off and watched in horror as her ball headed directly toward a group of men playing the next hole. The ball hit one of the men. He immediately clasped his hands together at his groin, fell to the ground and rolled around in agony.

The woman rushed up, and immediately began to apologize.

She said, "Please let me help. I'm a physical therapist and I know I could relieve your pain if you'd allow me."

"Oh, no, I'll be all right. I'll be fine in a few minutes," the man replied.

It was obvious that he was in agony, lying in the fetal position, still clasping his hands together at his groin.

The female golfer urged him to let him help him, so at her persistence, he allowed her to help.

She gently took his hands away and laid them to his side, loosened his trousers and put her hands inside. She administered tender and artful gentle massage to his privates.

Five minutes later the man was sighing with satisfaction when she asked, "How does that feel?"

He replied, "That feels great, but I think it's my right-hand thumb that really hurts."

Two friends were playing golf when one pulled out a cigar but he didn't have a lighter. So he asked his friend if he had one.

"I sure do," he replied, and reached into his golf bag and pulled out a foot long BIC lighter.

His friend asked, "Where did you get that whopper?"

"I got it from my genie."

"You have a genie?" the first guy asked.

"Yep, he's right here in my golf bag." He opens his golf bag and out pops a genie.

The friend says, "I'm a good friend of your master, will you grant me a wish?"

"Yes, I will," the genie replies.

So, the friend asks the genie for 'a million bucks.'

The genie replied, "It will be done."

He hops back into the golf bag and leaves the golfers standing there waiting for the 'million bucks.'

Suddenly the sky begins to darken and soon a million ducks surround the golfers.

"Hey," yells the disappointed golfer. "I asked your genie for a million bucks, not a million ducks."

"Sorry," the other golfer replied, "He's hard of hearing, and besides, do you really think that I'd ask a genie for a 12-inch BIC?"

A grandfather was at his grandson's wedding reception, giving him advice on having a happy marriage and a great life.

The young groom asked, "Grandfather, what's it like making love when you reach your age?"

The grandfather replied, "Well, it's kind of like putting with a rope."

A man got on a bus, with both of his trouser pockets full of golf balls, and sat down next to a beautiful blonde.

The blonde kept looking quizzically at him and his obviously bulging pants.

Finally, after a few glances from her, he said to her, "It's golf balls."

The blonde looked at him compassionately and said, "Oh you poor thing. I bet that hurts a lot more than tennis elbow."

Two couples were enjoying a competitive, best ball match, wives against husbands with the losers buying lunch and drinks.

On the final hole, the match was even and one of the wives had a long, breaking, fifteen foot putt to win the match. She lined the ball up carefully and confidently stroked the winning putt.

It was right on line, but unfortunately, it stopped three inches short of the hole.

Her husband thought that this was a riot and laughing said, "Right train, wrong ticket."

The wife failed to see the humor and not cracking a smile replied, "No sleeper cars on that train either."

Paul and Robert were enjoying a round of golf.

Robert had putted out at the eight green and had walked back to the cart. As Paul sank his putt, Robert suddenly jumped out of the cart and dropped his pants. He had just sat on a bee and got a nasty sting and desperately asked his partner to get the stinger out.

The sight of a man kneeling next to his playing partner's bare rear end was simply too much for the group playing behind them.

The group raced up to the two golfers and asked a single question, "What was the bet?"

A man was playing a round on his own. On the 15th tee he hooked his ball into some buttercups along the left of the fairway.

Being an honorable man, he penalized himself one stroke and moved his ball out of the pretty flowers.

A fairy then appeared and she said, "Thank you for moving your ball out of the earth's beautiful buttercups; you will now be blessed with an unlimited supply of butter for the rest of your life."

"Well, thanks," the man replied, "but where were you yesterday when I hit my ball into the pussywillows?"

You can re-work this gag, so that is you telling the story.

I played the course at County Hills the other day for the first time. On the 15th I hooked my drive into some buttercups.

I didn't want to damage the pretty little plants, so I took a drop and after I played my next shot, a fairy appeared.

She said to me, "Thank you for not damaging the buttercups. As your reward, you will now be blessed with an unlimited supply of butter for the rest of your life."

I said, "Thanks, but where were you on the previous hole when I hit my ball into the pussywillows?"

Mick won first prize at a Father's Day tournament which was an envelope.

When he opened the envelope, he was very surprised to find a voucher for a free visit to a brothel. He had never been to one before but he decided to go the next day even though he was very nervous.

The girls were very friendly and he soon found a young lady he fancied and he went with her to her room.

Ten minutes later, she came running back to the Madam and asked, "Can you tell me what a Mulligan is?"

Two women were playing golf and they came to a testing par 3.

The first woman hits her shot straight and the ball finishes in the middle of the green.

The second woman takes a solid swing and her ball lands on the green too and it finishes just one centimeter from the first ball.

The other woman says, "Wow. I've never seen two balls so close before."

Four married guys were golfing. While playing the 4th hole, the following conversation took place:

Chris says, "You have no idea what I had to do to be able to come out golfing this weekend. I had to promise my wife that I will paint the spare room next weekend."

Derek says, "That's nothing, I had to promise my wife I will build a patio."

Bryan says, "Man, you both have it easy! I had to promise my wife I will re-do the kitchen for her."

They continued to play the hole when they realized that Roy hadn't said anything. So they asked him, "You haven't said anything about what you had to do to be able to come golfing this weekend. What's the deal?"

Roy says, "You were lucky. I set my alarm for 6:30 a.m. and when it went off, I gave the wife a gentle nudge and said, 'golf course or intercourse?'"

She said, "Wear your sweater."

A couple of weeks ago, I played with a new member who shot an even par 72.

We had fun during the round, so I asked him if he wanted to play next week.

He said, "Sure, but I might be half an hour late."

The following week he shows up right on time, and sets up on the first tee this time playing left-handed – and again he shoots a 72.

I asked him if he wanted to play again next week.

He replied, "Sure but I might be half an hour late."

I then asked him, "How come sometimes you play right-handed and other times you play left-handed."

He said, "When I wake up in the morning and my wife is sleeping on her left side, I play left-handed and if she is on her right side, then I play right-handed."

I then asked, "So, what if she is lying flat on her back?"

He replied, "That's when I'll be half an hour late."

Sam and Rachel are having a drink toasting their 50th wedding anniversary.

Sam asks his wife, "Rachel, I was just wondering, have you ever cheated on me?"

Rachel replies, "Oh Sam, why would you ask me such a question after all these years? You really don't want to know the answer to that question."

Sam says, "Rachel, I really do want to know. In fact I insist. Darling please tell me if you have ever cheated on me."

Rachel replies, "Well, all right. Yes I have cheated, 3 times."

Sam is aghast and says, "Three? Well, when were they?"

Rachel replies, "Well, Sam, remember when you were 35 years old and you really wanted to start your own business and no bank would give you a loan? Remember, then one day the bank manager came over to the house and signed the loan papers?"

Sam says, "Oh, Rachel, you did that for me. I respect you even more than ever, to do such a thing for me. So, when was number 2?"

Rachel replies, "Well, Sam, remember a few years ago when you were really ill and you were in need of that operation, and the waiting list was months? Then remember how Dr. Harrison came all the way up here, and then you got booked in the following week?"

Sam says, "I can't believe that you should do such a thing for me, to save my life. I couldn't have a more wonderful wife. To do such a thing, you must really love me. So, when was number 3?"

Rachel replies, "Well, Sam, remember a few years ago, when you really wanted to be captain of the golf club and you were 5 votes short?"

A husband and wife are lying quietly in bed reading when the wife looks over at him and asks a question.

Wife: "Would you get married again if I died?"

Husband: "Definitely not, honey."

Wife: "Why not? Don't you like being married?"

Husband: "Of course I do."

Wife: "Then why wouldn't you remarry?"

Husband: "Okay, okay, - I'd get married again."

Wife: "Would you live in our house?"

Husband: "Sure - it's a great house."

Wife: "Would you sleep with her in our bed?"

Husband: "Where else would we sleep darling?"

Wife: "Would you replace my pictures with hers?"

Husband: "That would seem like the proper thing to do."

Wife: "Would you take her golfing with you?"

Husband: "Yes - Those are always good times."

Wife: "Would she use my clubs?"

Husband: "'No, she's left-handed."

Silence.

Husband: "Oh Damn!"

A keen golfer was involved in a nasty car crash and was rushed to hospital.

"I have some good news and some bad news for you," the surgeon told him. "The bad news is that I have to remove your right arm."

"Oh God no, my golfing days are over," cries the man. "So what is the good news?"

The surgeon replies, "The good news is that we have another arm available to replace it with, but it's a woman's arm so I will need your permission before I can go ahead with the transplant."

The man says, "As long as I can play golf again, let's do it, doc."

The operation went well and a year later the man went in for a check-up.

"How's the new arm?" asks the surgeon.

"Just great," says the golfer. "I'm playing the best golf of my life. My new arm has a much finer touch, and my putting has really improved."

"Not only that," continued the golfer, "my handwriting has improved, I've learned how to sew my own clothes and I've even taken up painting landscapes in watercolors."

The surgeon said, "Are you having any side effects?"

"Well, just two" said the golfer, "I have trouble parking the car and, every time I get an erection, I also get a headache."

Why Golf Is Better Than Sex

- You don't have to sneak your golf magazines into the house.

- If you are having trouble with golf, it is perfectly acceptable to pay a professional to show you how to improve your technique.

- If your partner takes pictures or videotapes of you golfing, you don't have to worry about them showing up on the Internet.

- Your golf partner won't keep asking questions about other partners you've golfed with.

- It's perfectly respectable to golf with a total stranger.

- When you see a really good golfer, you don't have to feel guilty about imagining the two of you golfing together.

- If your regular golf partner isn't available, he/she won't object if you golf with someone else.

- Nobody will ever tell you that you will go blind if you golf by yourself.

- You don't have to go to a sleazy shop in a seedy neighborhood to buy golf stuff.

- You can have a golf calendar on your wall at the office.

- There is no such thing as a golfing transmitted disease.

- The Ten Commandments do not say anything about golf.

- If you want to watch golf on television, you don't have to subscribe to a premium TV channel.

- Nobody expects you to promise to golf with just one partner for the rest of your life.

- Nobody expects you to give up golfing if your partner loses interest in the game.

- You don't have to be a newlywed to plan a vacation primarily for the enjoyment of golf.

- Your golf partner will never say, "We had golf last week. Is that all you ever think about?"

If you enjoyed the rude jokes in this chapter, you may wish to track down my "Adult Golf Jokes" book on Amazon.

As the name of the book implies, it has many, many adult themed golf gags, and they are much ruder than these.

Chapter 7: Golf Quotes

"Golf is like a love affair. If you don't take it seriously, it's no fun; if you take it seriously, it will break your heart." *Arthur Daley*

"To find a man's true character, play golf with him." *P.G. Wodehouse*

"If you find golf relaxing, you're not doing it right." *Bob Hope*

"Golf is a game whose aim is to hit a very small ball, into an even smaller hole, with weapons ill designed for that purpose." *Winston Churchill*

"One good thing about the rain in Scotland is that most of it ends up as Scotch." *Peter Alliss.*

"Thinking instead of acting is the number one golf disease." *Sam Snead.*

"The older I get, the better I used to be." *Lee Trevino*

"Golf is flog spelled backwards." *Milton Berle*

"Golf is played mainly on a five and a half inch course; the distance between your ears." *Bobby Jones*

"There are two things you can do with your head down, play golf and pray." *Lee Trevino*

"Golf is a game in which you claim the privileges of age and retain the playthings of youth." *Samuel Johnson*

"Find a man with both feet firmly on the ground and you've found a man about to make a difficult putt." *Fletcher Knebel*

"A game in which a ball 1 1/2 inches in diameter is played on a ball 8,000 miles in diameter. The object is to hit the small ball, but not the larger." *John Cunningham*

"Golf is the most fun you can have without taking your clothes off." *Chi Chi Rodriguez*

"I can air mail the golf ball, but sometimes I don't put the right address on it." *Jim Dent*

"Golf gives you an insight into human nature, your own as well as your opponent's." *Grantland Rice*

"The loudest sound you hear is the guy jingling coins to distract a player he bet against." *Jim Murray*

"The IRS has made liars out of more Americans than the game of golf." *Will Rogers*

"I used to play golf with a guy who cheated so badly that he once had a hole-in-one and wrote down zero on the scorecard." *Bob Bruce*

"Golf is a compromise between what your ego wants you to do, what experience tells you to do, and what your nerves tell you to do." *Bruce Crampton*

"If you drink, don't drive. Don't even putt." *Dean Martin*

"Golf is a game you play with your own worst enemy - yourself." *Finley Peter Dunne*

"I asked my caddie for a sand wedge and he came back in ten minutes with a ham on rye sandwich." *Chi Chi Rodriguez (on his accent.)*

"Golf is a plague invented by Calvinist Scots as a punishment for man's sins." *James Reston*

"Why am I using a new putter? Because the last one didn't float very well." *Dougie Terrie*

"The greatest thing about golf, there's no end to it unless you're dead." *Fuzzy Zoeller*

"I'd give up golf if I didn't have so many sweaters." *Bob Hope*

"I'm not saying my golf game went bad, but if I grew tomatoes, they'd come up sliced." *Lee Trevino*

"I don't like to watch golf on television. I hate all that whispering." *Trevor Wood*

"You can always spot the employee playing golf with his boss. He's the fellow who birdies a hole and says, "oops!"" *Bob Monkhouse*

"I'm hitting the woods just great, but I'm having a dreadful time getting out of them." *Nigel Greene*

"Golf is the only game I know where a man aged 60 can beat a man aged 30." *Carl Christensen*

"You can talk to a fade, but a hook won't listen." *Lee Trevino*

"Golf always makes me so damned angry." *King George V.*

"If you can break 100, watch your golf. If you can break 80, watch your business." *Joey Adams*

"If you are going to throw a club, throw it down the fairway in front of you. That way you don't waste energy going to pick it up." *Tommy Bolt*

"Never bet with anyone you meet on the first tee who has a deep suntan, a 1-iron in his bag, and squinty eyes." *Davey Marr*

"The uglier a man's legs are, the better he plays golf. It's almost a law." *H.G. Wells*

"They say Sam Snead is a natural golfer. But if he did not practice, he'd be a natural bad golfer." *Gary Player*

"I regularly enjoy a round or two at my golf club. I sometimes play golf too." *Ronnie Barker*

"I had a wonderful experience on the golf course today. I had a hole in nothing. Missed the ball and sank the divot." *Don Adams*

"I'm convinced the reason most people play golf is to wear clothes they would not otherwise be caught dead in." *Roger Simon*

"Isn't it fun to go out on the golf course and lie in the sun." *Bob Hope*

"No matter how good you get you can always get better and that's the exciting part." *Tiger Woods*

"Golf is meaningless; but it means so much." *Paolo Hoskinson*

"Golf is a young man's vice and an old man's penance." *Irvin S. Cobb*

"It's good sportsmanship not to pick up lost balls while they are still rolling." *Dave Bunting*

"Golf without bunkers would be tame and monotonous. As would life." *B.C. Forbes*

"It takes a lot of balls to play golf the way I do." *Shaun Cavaghan*

"The only time my prayers are never answered is on the golf course." *Billy Graham*

"Golf is a game in which you yell 'fore,' shoot six, and write down five." *Paul Harvey*

"Golf is so popular simply because it is the best game in the world at which to be bad." *A. A. Milne*

"I play golf with friends, but to me there are no such things as friendly games." *Shamus MacDonald*

"I regard golf as an expensive way of playing marbles." *G.K. Chesterton*

"Golf is played by millions of American men whose wives think they are out having fun." *Jim Bishop*

"The object of a bunker or a trap is not only to punish a physical mistake, to punish lack of control, but also to punish pride and egotism." *Charles B. McDonald*

"I go into the woods so often, I can tell you which plants are edible." *Roy Jones*

"I know I am getting better at golf because I am hitting fewer spectators." *Gerald R. Ford*

"Although golf was originally restricted to wealthy, overweight Protestants, today it's open to anybody who owns hideous clothing." *Dave Barry*

"If you are caught on a golf course during a storm and are afraid of lightning, hold up a 1-iron. Not even God can hit a 1-iron." *Lee Trevino*

"I have a tip that can take five strokes off anyone's game; it's called an eraser." *Arnold Palmer*

"I always thought of myself as some sort of athlete until I started playing golf a couple years ago." *James Caan*

"Golf was my first glimpse of comedy. I was a caddie when I was a kid." *Bill Murray*

"If people gripped a knife and fork the way they do a golf club, they'd starve to death." *Sam Snead*

"Show me a man who is a good loser and I'll show you a man who is playing golf with his boss." *James Patrick Murray*

"He who has the fastest golf cart never has a bad lie." *Mickey Mantle*

"Mistakes are part of the game. It's how well you recover from them, that's the mark of a great player." *Alice Cooper*

"I was so bad at golf they would have to check me for ticks at the end of the round because I'd spent half the day in the woods." *Jeff Foxworthy*

"The most important shot in golf is the next one." *Ben Hogan*

"Don't hurry; don't worry, and be sure to smell the flowers along the way." *Walter Hagen*

"As you walk down the fairway of life, you must smell the roses, for you only get to play one round." *Ben Hogan*

"My best score is 103, but I've only been playing for 15 years." *Alex Karras*

"Golf is the infallible test. The man who can go into a patch of rough alone, with the knowledge that only God is watching him, and play his ball where it lies, is the man who will serve you faithfully and well." *P.G. Wodehouse*

"Every day you miss practising will take you one day longer to be good." *Ben Hogan*

"The harder I practise the luckier I get." *Gary Player*

"Golf is a good walk spoiled." *Mark Twain*

"Golf is a game that is played on a five-inch course – the distance between your ears." *Bobby Jones*

Chapter 8: Golf Parables

Golf can best be defined as an endless series of tragedies obscured by the occasional miracle, followed by a cold beer or two.

Golf is the only sport where the most feared opponent is yourself.

Golf is an odd game. You hit down to make the ball go up. You swing left and the ball goes right. The lowest score wins. On top of all that, the winner buys the drinks.

Golf is like marriage. Both are expensive and if you take yourself too seriously, you're in trouble.

Golfers who try to make everything perfect before taking their shot rarely make a perfect shot.

A man goes to a clairvoyant, who tells him, "I see lots of sand, trees and water. You must be a golfer."

The term 'mulligan' is really a contraction of the phrase 'maul it again.'

A 'gimme' can best be defined as an agreement between two golfers; neither of whom can putt very well.

No matter how badly you play, it is always possible to get worse.

Golf is like fishing in that both mysteriously encourage exaggeration.

Golf is a hard game to figure out. One day you'll slice it and shank it, hit into all the traps and miss every green. The next day you go out and for no reason at all you will be completely useless.

If your best shots are the practice swing and the 'gimme putt', you might wish to reconsider this game.

The only reason I play golf is to bug my wife. She thinks I'm having fun.

I wish I could play my normal game. Just once.

It's not whether you win or lose that counts, it's whether I win or lose.

Golf is 90% mental, which is why the people I play with think I'm crazy.

The Range:- A place where golfers go to convert a nasty hook into a wicked slice.

A male golfer is often a confused soul who talks about women when he's playing golf, and about golf when he's with a woman.

In golf, some people tend to get confused with numbers. They shoot a "six", yell "fore" and write "five".

Old golfers never die, they just lose their balls.

The position of your hands is very important when playing golf. I use mine to cover up my scorecard.

It's amazing how a golfer who never helps out around the house will replace his divots, repair his ball marks, and rake the sand traps.

Many golfers have two handicaps: one for bragging and one for betting.

When you stop to think about it, have you noticed that it's a lot easier to get up at 6am to play golf than at 10am to go shopping?

Golf is by far the ultimate love / hate relationship. Sometimes it seems as though your cup runneth over.

It takes longer to learn good golf than it does brain surgery. On the other hand, you don't get to ride around on a cart, drink beer, eat hot dogs and fart while performing brain surgery.

A good drive on the 18th hole has stopped many a golfer from giving up the game.

Golf is the perfect thing to do on Sunday because you always end up praying a lot.

A good golf partner is one who's always slightly worse than you.

Let's finish with this - A bad day at golf is better than a good day at work.

White And Dimpled

In my hand I hold a ball,
White and dimpled, rather small
Oh, how bland it does appear,
This harmless looking little sphere.

By its size I could not guess,
The awesome strength it does possess
But since I fell beneath its spell,
I've wandered through the fires of Hell.

My life has not been quite the same,
Since I chose to play this game
It rules my mind for hours on end,
A fortune it has made me spend.

It has made me curse and cry,
I hate myself and want to die
It promises a thing called "par",
If I can hit it straight and far.

To master such a tiny ball,
Should not be very hard at all
But my desires the ball refuses,
And does exactly as it chooses.

It hooks and slices, dribble and dies,
Or disappears before my eyes
Often it will have a whim,
To hit a tree or take a swim.

With miles of grass on which to land,
It finds a tiny patch of sand
Then has me offering up my soul,
If it will just drop in the hole.

It's made me whimper like a pup,
And swear that I will give it up
And take a drink to ease my sorrow,
But "The Ball" knows - I'll be back tomorrow.

You Know You're A Golfaholic If....

You think that one day you'll shoot your age, when a more realistic goal would be to shoot your weight.

You know there's more to life than golf, but you're not interested in finding out what it is.

You quit the game forever, twice a month.

You buy every new golf gizmo that comes out.

You think you're skilful and everybody else is lucky.

You miss the ball, but still think it was a great swing.

The new clubs you just bought cost more than your monthly mortgage payment.

You can't break 100 but still think you could give a pro a few tips.

Here's a slice of golf history to explain why there are 18 holes on a golf course, and not 10 or 20 or any other number.

During a discussion among the membership board at St. Andrews Golf Club in 1858, one of the members pointed out that it takes exactly 18 holes to polish off a fifth of Scotch.

By limiting himself to one shot of Scotch per hole, the wily old Scot figured a round of golf was finished when the Scotch ran out.

After a three year study, the National Science Foundation announced the following results on America's recreational preferences:

The sport of choice for unemployed or incarcerated people is basketball.

The sport of choice for maintenance level workers is bowling.

The sport of choice for blue-color workers is football.

The sport of choice for supervisors is baseball.

The sport of choice for middle management is tennis.

The sport of choice for corporate officers is golf.

The conclusion of the study was that the higher you rise up the corporate ladder the smaller your balls become.

Twelve Golf Citations

1) The number one thing about trouble is don't get into more.

2) Golf is unlike other sports. There's not a lot of point to it unless someone suffers, even if it's you.

3) The trees taunt you; the sand mocks you; the water calls your name; and they say golf is a quiet game.

4) Why is it that when you tell yourself, "Don't hit it into the water," you only hear the word 'water'?

5) It's a simple matter to keep your ball in the fairway if you're not choosy about which fairway.

6) "Fore!" is not an excuse. "So what?" is not an apology, and "Up yours" is not an explanation.

7) If profanity had any influence on the flight of a ball, most golfers would play a lot better.

8) A "gimme" is an agreement between two guys who can't putt.

9) Half of golf is fun. The other half is putting.

10) My favorite shots are the practice swing and the conceded putt.

11) If God didn't want man to have mulligans, balls wouldn't come three to a sleeve.

12) All I've got against golf is that it takes you too far from the clubhouse.

Chapter 9: Golf Slang

Golfers can be quite creative when describing some of their shots, or their partner's shots. Try and remember some of these for when you are out playing in the next few weeks.

Slang - Tee Shots

A Sally Gunnell	Ugly to look at, but a good runner
A Paula Radcliffe	Not as ugly as a Sally Gunnell and runs a long way
A Glenn Miller	Didn't make it over the water
An O.J. Simpson	Got away with it
A Gay Midget	It's low and it sucks
A Princess Grace	Should have taken a driver
A Princess Diana	Shouldn't have taken a driver
A Robert Downey Jr	A real snorter
A Condom	Safe but unsatisfying
A Posh Spice	Too thin
A Danny DeVito	Short and fat
A Giraffe's Arse	High and shitty
A Pavarotti	Sounded great but died
A Lindsay Lohan	Started straight but bent into the rough

A Gerry Adams	A provisional
A Tony Hart	Drawing
A Jean-Marie Le Pen	Too far right
A Ken Livingstone	Too far left
An Arthur Scargill	Great strike but a poor result
A Kerry Katona	High
A Richard Hammond	Veers off into the rough at speed
A Forrest Gump	Just keeps on running
An Oscar Bravo	OB – Out Of Bounds
A George Bush	Your dad could do better
A Mike Tyson	Punched it low
An Alex Ferguson	Heading straight for the drink
An Arsene Wenger	Everyone saw where it went except you
An Obi-Wan Kenobi	Out of bounds

Slang - Approach Shots

A Kate Winslet	A bit fat, but not too bad
A Kate Moss	A bit thin
A Circus Tent	A big top
A German Virgin	Guten tight – close to the pin
A Marc Bolan	Hit a tree
A Nipple Licker	A shot that opens up the hole
A Yasser Arafat	Ugly and in the sand
A Rick Waller	One club too many
A Jo Brand	Fat and ugly
A Beyoncé	Chunky but on the dance floor
A Rodney King	Overclubbed
A Roseanne Barr	Fat and short
A Bin Laden	In the water, lost forever
A Vinnie Jones	Got a nasty kick
Anna Kournikova	Looks great, but unlikely to get a result
A mother-in-law	It looks good when it's leaving
A son-in-law	Not what you wanted but it will have to do
A sister-in-law	You're up there although you know you shouldn't be

Slang - Putting

A James Joyce	A difficult read
A J R Tolkien	A great read
Salman Rushdie	An impossible read
A Ray Charles	Didn't see the break
A Bon Jovi	Half way there
A Cuban	Needed another revolution
A Rock Hudson	Thought it was straight but it wasn't
A Joe Pesci	A mean little five footer
A Danny DeVito	An ugly little five footer
A Maradona	A nasty little five footer
Monica Lewinsky	Lipped out
A Brazilian	Shaves the hole
An Elton John	A big bender that lips the rim
Lipstick on a pig	Holing a long putt after some previous dross

You're dancing, but there's no music playing...You're on the green but a long way from the flag.

Slang - On The Course

A Paris Hilton	An expensive hole
A Simon Cowell	Needs to be hit really hard
An OJ Simpson	Blame the golf glove
A Pippa Middleton	You just want to smack it
A Linda Rondstadt	Blew by you (Blue Bayou)
A Tommy Sheridan	A shocking lie
A Dead Sheep	Still ewe
Tee Way Back	Chinese for a long hole
Ben Hogan to Hulk Hogan	Playing like God but then went absolute crap
Cream on sh*t	Scrambling a par after many bad shots
A Ladyboy	Looks like an easy hole but all is not what it seems

Slang - In A Hazard

An Adolf Hitler   Two shots in a bunker
An Eva Braun   Picked up in a bunker
A Saddam Hussein   Go from bunker to bunker
A Red October   Underwater
A Bigfoot   Stumbling out of the woods
A Chuck Berry   Blocked out
                       no particular place to go

Slang - Scoring

A Snowman   8 shots on a hole
A Beethoven   9 shots on a hole
A Bo Derek   10 shots on a hole
A Paris Hilton   An expensive hole
A Spaniard   Four for four
(Stableford - 4 strokes for 4 points)

Chapter 10: Golfers Pick-Up Lines

Which do you prefer? Stroke Play or Skins?

I hope you like it rough.

From the moment I saw you, I've had a vertical shaft angle.

Bring some friends, and we can play a foursome.

I have a stiff shaft.

I have a pretty good swing.

Hey baby, can you suck a golf ball through 50 feet of garden hose?

Are you looking for the fairway? Because you coming back to my place is the only fair way for this evening to go.

My balls are always clean.

Are you into kinky stuff? Would you like to do something I won't do for anyone else. I'll let you beat me.

I am good with my approach play.

How many strokes do you want?

I can grip it and rip it.

I have an extra-long shaft.

It looks pretty wet down there.

Keep your head down and spread your legs a bit.

I am looking for a new partner for regular match ups.

Chapter 11: Bumper Stickers For Golfers

My balls have dimples.

Think I'm a lousy driver? Wait until you see me putt.

Sometimes I think I'm really a great golfer. Other times I'm sober.

May the course be with you.

Yes, I have a retirement plan. I plan to play golf.

Golf is my therapy.

Born to play golf. Forced to work.

I'd rather be driving a golf ball.

Eat. Sleep. Golf. Repeat.

I'd rather be golfing.

The Golf Father.

I golf, therefore I am.

Chapter 12: Kids Jokes

Q: What do you call a lion playing golf?
A: *Roarin' McIlroy.*

Q: Why do sensible golfers wear two pairs of socks?
A: *In case they get a hole in one.*

Q: Where do ghosts play golf?
A: *On a golf corpse.*

Q: Why can't Tiger Woods listen to music?
A: *Because he broke the records.*

Q: Where can you find a golfer on a Saturday night?
A: *Clubbing.*

Q: What does a golfer do on his day off?
A: *Putter around.*

Q: What did the dentist say to the golfer after examining his teeth?

A: *You have a hole in one.*

Q: What's a golfer's favorite letter?

A: *Tee.*

Q: Why do golfers hate cake?

A: *Because they might get a slice.*

Q: Why don't golfers in England work in the afternoon?

A: *Because it would interrupt their tee time.*

Q: What is a golfer's favorite type of flower?

A: *Fore-get-me-nots.*

Q: Why was the computer so good at golf?

A: *Because it had a hard drive.*

Q: What time is it when an elephant steps on your golf ball?

A: *Time to get a new ball.*

Q: Why didn't the skeleton play golf?

A: *His heart wasn't in it.*

Q: Have you always been a bad golfer?

A: *It's a fore-gone conclusion.*

Q: How many golfers does it take to change a light bulb?

A: *FORE.*

Q: What did one golf ball say to the other golf ball?

A: *See you around.*

Q: Why was Cinderella such a poor golfer?

A: *Her coach was a pumpkin.*

Q: Why did they kick Tarzan off the golf course?

A: *He screamed with every swing.*

Did you hear about the Mexican golfer who got shot yesterday?

The detectives said it was a hole in Juan.

A golf club walks into a local bar and asks the barman for a pint of beer.

The barman refuses to serve him.

"Why not?" asks the golf club.

"You'll be driving later," replies the barman.

Two young boys are playing marbles when one of them missed an easy shot, and swore.

His mother protested saying, "What do little boys who swear when they are playing marbles turn into?"

Her son replied, "Golfers!"

About The Author

Chester Croker, known to his friends as Chester the Jester, has written many joke books, and has twice been awarded Comedy Writer of the Year by the International Jokers Guild. In over 30 years playing golf, Chester has met many funny characters that have helped provide him with plenty of material for this book.

Hopefully, you have enjoyed this book and it has added a few gems to your repertoire of golf jokes.

If you have seen anything wrong in this book, or have a gag you would like to see included in the next version of the book, please visit the glowwormpress.com website and send me a message.

If you enjoyed the book, please review it on Amazon so that other golfers can have a good laugh too.

The final word:-

Let's remember that golf is a game invented by the same people who think that music comes out of a bagpipe.

Made in the USA
Las Vegas, NV
03 December 2020